THE MARTIAL ARTS
COACHING MANUAL

THE MARTIAL ARTS COACHING MANUAL

A MARTIAL ARTS COMMISSION APPROVED BOOK

DAVID MITCHELL

A & C BLACK · LONDON

First published 1988 by
A & C Black (Publishers) Limited
35 Bedford Row, London WC1R 4JH

© 1988 David Mitchell

ISBN 0 7136 5625 5

British Library Cataloguing in Publication Data
Mitchell, David, 1944–
    The martial arts coaching manual.
    1. Martial arts
    I. Title
796.8
    ISBN 0–7136–5625–5

Printed and bound in Great Britain by
Mackays of Chatham PLC

CONTENTS

ACKNOWLEDGEMENTS

Many people have contributed towards my interest in, and knowledge of, coaching and it gives me great pleasure to place on record my thanks to the following:

Doctor James Canney, the Martial Arts Commission Medical Officer, for permission to quote from his excellent lectures;

Tony Gummerson, the senior lecturer in Exercise Physiology at the College of Ripon & York (Tony acted as major reviewer and contributor);

Rex Hazeldine, the Deputy Director of the National Coaching Foundation, for his enthusiasm and advice over the years;

John White, a National Coach of the British Amateur Gymnastics Association, for several tips on warm-up;

Rick Schofield of the British Kendo Association for his lecture on Learning Theory;

Gill Canney, a physiotherapist with firm views on the need to protect joints before they're injured!;

The National Coaching Foundation for their excellent resource materials.

INTRODUCTION

I had been training in the martial arts for about 22 years when I first came into contact with coaching. At the time I was both General Secretary of the Martial Arts Commission and a senior martial art instructor with practical experience at producing dan grades. I had never been taught how to pass on the skills I had acquired and wasn't sure how non-martial artists could make me into a better instructor.

So, more out of curiosity than anything else, I persuaded the honorary officers to agree to a series of seminars covering aspects of coaching. They took place over a bleak off-season weekend in Blackpool. Since I wasn't convinced the seminars would be either interesting or relevant, I decided to play safe and invite Doctor Jim Canney to give one of his popular lectures on martial art injuries. That at least would be worth going for.

No offence to Jim, but I needn't have bothered! As it was, there wasn't enough time to do justice to the coaching topics. The first lecturer was Tony Gummerson from Leeds and within seconds he had captured the complete attention of the highly graded audience by simply asking them, 'How do you *know* that you're a good coach?'

By the end of that particular lecture, I wondered whether I'd really been such a hot-shot teacher all those years. However, Tony told us that we probably weren't totally useless, though it had taken us a couple of decades to get to our present level of teaching expertise. The idea of coach training, we learned, was to produce good coaches in considerably less time than that!

The second lecturer was Rex Hazeldine from Loughborough and, though less controversial, he intrigued the audience with his description of fitness.

At the end of the weekend, a senior martial art instructor came to me and said 'I wish to God I'd known about all this 20 years ago!' For me, that said it all.

The Blackpool Seminar marked the beginning of a widespread coaching development within the Martial Arts Commission and it was soon followed by others. At first, we decided to cast our net wide, so as to find out which topics were relevant and which were not. We also began to build links between general aspects of coaching and applications specific to our martial art practice. That process is still going on today.

As you will have gathered, the idea of formalised coaching as we now understand it had come late to the martial arts practised in Britain. Most of the arts have been in the U.K. for more than twenty years, whilst two were established more than forty years ago. The reticence to adopt western principles of coaching was derived from a number of factors, all of which had to be taken into account when adapting coaching principles to suit martial art practice.

The martial arts were not devised with a sporting connotation in mind. Originally, they were military and fighting techniques intended to help the user survive a hostile encounter. By and large the techniques practised were known to work, otherwise their originators would have perished! Moreover, martial art instructors themselves had passed the test of combat and had survived. Worthwhile new techniques were incorporated into the school training manual and were taught as a system of practice known as 'The Syllabus'.

Circumstances change in martial arts as they do in most other things and some techniques became obsolete as new weapons and circumstances superseded the old ones. The obsolete systems often continued to be practised, but for different purposes. Techniques no longer needed to be purely practical, so other emphases developed. Some schools concentrated largely on combat sport aspects, whilst others used training to improve the character.

In many traditional schools, the instructor worked with only 1 or 2 students, allowing complicated techniques to be taught. In contrast, a large class requires those same techniques to be broken down into smaller sub-units and it is because of this that the very structure of martial arts in Britain and elsewhere has changed. Novice martial artists in the West regard practice in the same way as any other leisure activity. Their attitude differs markedly from Far Eastern students who seem to have a greater motivation towards intense practice. This latter attitude has resulted in a form of élitist coaching designed to weed out those who will not make the standard imposed by the school.

In some schools, the novice was given no instruction whatsoever but was left to copy the seniors. If he was lucky, from time to time someone might correct a few of his glaring errors. This correction was often made in a brutal way – openings in stance, for example, were pointed out with a hard kick or punch. Other schools deliberately tried to drive novices away by giving them repeated beatings.

This method of teaching was introduced to Britain by visiting instructors and I personally witnessed some of the training methods referred to above. Lining up with all the other grades to take a bashing from the instructor became a regular part of practice. Grading examinations were tests of endurance and no one felt he had earned a grade unless he suffered for it.

The majority of novices left such clubs within 3 months of joining and there is no doubt in my mind that this form of training was a major contributor to the very high turnover of students in the martial arts. On the other hand, the system did produce a small number of good quality martial artists.

In contrast to the situation in the Far East, much money can be made in the West from teaching martial arts. The more students there are paying affiliations and training fees over a longer period, the more prosperous is the club. On the other hand, if training intensity is reduced so that more students stay (and pay) for longer, then general standards fall. This is the dilemma facing the martial arts. My personal answer to this dilemma is to stream classes so they accommodate both large numbers of average achievers and a small number of élite performers. The finances gained from the large class can be used to pay for extra time spent on the élite group.

Having said that, I do not presume to tell you how to run your particular martial art club. But what I can tell you is that regardless of the path you elect to follow, the application of coaching principles will improve the training you give.

Consider firstly how these principles have affected national and international competition. The old idea was to get your team into a minibus at about 4.00 a.m. on the day of competition, drive 200 miles to Crystal Palace and take part in a national competition. The same procedure applied for international events. By comparison, the results of correctly preparing a well selected team are never more clearly seen than in British karate where, at the time of writing, the team has won four world team championships – the last three consecutively.

Then apply coaching principles to traditional training which has otherwise tended to throw out the baby with the bathwater. This is because such training is geared towards producing eastern martial artists. Is it not our aim to develop tough, highly-motivated and analytical martial artists who surpass their eastern counterparts? If the answer is yes, then we must use training methods which better suit western practitioners. These need not be less arduous than eastern methods but must be more effective. Let me give an example.

I began my martial art training under a Japanese 7th dan black belt. He taught using traditional methods and when I asked him to recommend a hip-flexibility improvement exercise, he advised me to buy a pair of iron sandles, strap them onto my feet and then repeatedly kick as high and hard as I could! I now know that given to a novice, that advice was at best ineffective and at worst positively harmful. The correct training approach for traditional martial arts first recognises the need to maintain purity of technique and then goes on to teach that technique as effectively as possible. Where it is necessary to test the students' determination, the coach will increase meaningful training pressure whilst monitoring its effects. By this means, a greater number of good students will make it into the higher grades and a higher proportion of those will cross over from mere technician to true martial artist.

Some traditional teachers claim that coaching principles cannot be applied to martial arts which contain no sporting aspect. However, in the broadest sense of the word, all martial arts contain an element of competition if only through the struggle to exceed yesterday's standards. Whatever the motives for this struggle – be they to defeat an opponent, to win a selection, to obtain a desired grading, or simply to attain a higher plane of philosophical understanding – an element of competition is there.

For those who prefer teaching larger classes containing many lower level performers, the application of coaching principles will help them attract more students, and keep those they have for a longer period, whilst improving overall performances in both gradings and competition. It will do this by giving them a new insight into training methods; varying lessons in content and work level; and pacing students so a good performance occurs on the day of grading/competition. Students will feel they are progressing and will be motivated to try that bit harder. Despite all this, there are still some senior instructors who remain unconvinced. I am sure that the majority of these have the same opinion I in my ignorance held before the Blackpool seminar. 'What can anyone teach *me* about my martial art?' The answer is quite simply, nothing at all, but that is not what coaching courses set out to do anyway. What they will do is help a coach communicate more effectively the principles of his martial art.

Many of those of us who started martial art in the early 1960s did not have the benefit of training under good coaches and, in consequence, can remember the good students who dropped out as a result of needless injury and inapplicable coaching philosophy. It is up to us now to ensure that our students receive better guidance.

Don't expect coaching to provide every answer. Coaches are all learning together and improvements come about through assessments, research, seminars and discussions. This is a continuous process and one to which you, as a coach, can contribute.

Throughout the book coaches and students are, in the main, referred to individually as 'he'. This should, of course, be taken to mean 'he or she' where appropriate. In conclusion, let me leave you with a summary:

Skill in martial art + knowledge of coaching principles = better students in every way.

David Mitchell
Penrith

THE REQUIREMENTS OF A GOOD MARTIAL ARTS COACH

The benefits of good coaching

You might think that all a coach does is teach technique but actually there is much more to it than that. For example, a well coached martial art benefits health, whilst poor coaching can cause long-term serious damage.

Good coaching generates a positive self-esteem amongst students, whilst poor coaching produces arrogance and bullying. Students who are self-motivated through good coaching train more effectively and more fully accept disciplined practice.

The skill requirement

Good martial art coaches are not created overnight. One of the two basic requirements takes years to meet, and here I am referring to skill. I have been told that in one or two other activities a coach can qualify without ever having been a good performer. This is not the case in martial arts, although when they were in their British infancy it was expedient to use low grades to teach. Thankfully, circumstances have changed and there are now enough high grades about to qualify as full coaches.

Novices quickly pick up bad habits and poor technique if their teacher has insufficient technical skill to recognise and correct faults. These errors are difficult to eradicate later in the novices' training. So, whilst sending low grades to a coaching course may result in personnel who are more adept at communicating the wrong messages to the class, they will at least become able to recognise unsafe practices. Therefore, whilst it is not a good idea to delegate the running of clubs to low grades, if such delegation is essential for the wellbeing of a young and expanding association, then coach training will not make matters worse.

The good coach must have followed the same training as the students, because though a technique may look simple to perform it takes years of experience for its meaning and application to become clear. No manual can adequately explain those slight variations which transform a mildly effective technique into a masterful one. Through properly supervised practice, the technique itself is transcended and only then does the student become a potential teacher of others.

Surprisingly perhaps, it helps if the candidate coach has never been a natural performer. This is because gifted martial artists seem to do things right without ever knowing why or how. I well remember enrolling a student of dance into my club. She showed an amazing aptitude for duplicating any martial art technique shown to her and within 6 weeks she could repeat the contents of an average year's syllabus. She left shortly afterwards and deprived the martial arts of a future Rosy Lee (Bruce Lee's sister)! I suppose it might have been that things came too easy: there was no challenge and little motivation.

At the other extreme, one of my students was the most unco-ordinated and least supple of any young men I ever coached. He failed his novice grade on the first attempt and just managed to scrape through into a third-class grade on his second attempt. Three months later he failed his examination for the next grade, but was content to have raised his skill so that it just tipped into a second-class novice grade. He also failed on his second attempt, but inched his way into a first-class novice grade. Finally, he scraped through into his second grade, when the process was repeated. This happened in all 8 grades to the black belt and the process took him 13 years as opposed to the average 5.

Everything had to be explained in detail, then repeated and repeated again. I didn't mind spending time with him because he had such great motivation; it made me feel rather humble. He never complained when students who joined later beat him into the high grades and it is a tribute to his dedication that he finally reached the necessary skill level for a black belt award.

He now runs a club and is a very successful teacher. There is nothing he doesn't know about technique and, after taking a coaching course, I know he'll make one of Britain's best coaches.

An outlook on coaching

Along with the arduous training needed to attain a high enough skill level comes an equally important factor: outlook on practice. This outlook develops as a result of the way students have been taught, the philosophy of the schools in which they practise and the goal they wish to obtain. A sense of pride in one's school is both inevitable and desirable, but a narrow and channelled outlook can also have a negative effect on students.

Consider the case of a colleague who believes that the sole purpose for studying karate is simply to be able to beat other people more effectively. He is dismissive of other styles and is critical of alternative stated objectives, saying 'That's all very well – but it isn't karate'. This attitude has impressed itself on his students who, as a result, are developing a similar outlook.

I regard this in the same light as the coach who perhaps has a favourite throwing technique and pushes it at every student regardless of individual capabilities. Such a coach is not capitalising upon the individual strengths and weaknesses of students, but is seeking instead to make them into clones of himself. The good coach knows his students and will not try to force them into areas for which they have no aptitude or inclination. Insensitive coaching in this respect has driven away many otherwise good students.

To counter a narrow approach, the martial art coach must be widely informed about other martial arts – not just to be able to sneer at them but to have a genuine appreciation of their practice. It is a fact that no single martial art is better than all the rest, though there may be one that is best for you personally.

Chinese and Okinawan teachers were long aware how valuable the study of other martial arts could be and sent promising students to other teachers to learn aspects of their practice. One teacher might be famed for his hand techniques, another for his wrist-locks; by training with both, the students developed an all-round excellence. Sadly, this is rare in the present day and age and even when it does occur it is sometimes misunderstood. I well remember another colleague telling me how a noted Okinawan karate teacher once trained at the headquarters of a different school. My colleague mistakenly thought he had given up his original practice to follow this other way.

A good coach will send students to other schools where they will benefit because:

1   the main obligation of a good coach is directed towards the students – not towards himself. He must act in their best interests at all times
2   the most important obligations of the student are respect for the coach, loyalty to the school and dedication to its form of practice. If students are not respectful, loyal or dedicated, then they are better off joining another club.

Though loyalty is a cornerstone of martial art practice, it is a much devalued currency in some schools nowadays. To some extent this is due to the Far Eastern founders who, whilst talking about the need to suppress the ego, found time to disagree so fundamentally on certain issues as to necessitate forming an alternative school of martial art. This process did not halt when it came to the West, although the reason for splintering is now other than one founded on philosophical grounds. It is responsible for a drop in the quality of martial art practice as founders of new schools split off at ever lower skill levels.

The history of the martial arts in Britain records a persistent and totally unsuccessful series of attempts to halt splintering. Different governing bodies have failed to come to terms with the fact that disaffected coaches cannot be forced to remain in membership of their parent association. If they remain, they act as foci of discontent and if expelled, they then become free of all responsibility to the ex-parent body.

If conciliation is not possible, then chief coaches are advised to face up to the facts and help the disaffected parties to re-settle themselves elsewhere.

Theoretically at least, the good coach need never face the trauma of splintering if he carefully selects his students, coaches and senior coaches; keeps his lines of communication short; is recognised as the source of all technical advancement; and clearly runs things for the benefit of the membership. Contrast this with a diffuse association of clubs, whose affiliation, grading and mat fees all flow one way, and where the head of school is seldom seen. Which of these two models is more likely to face splintering?

Are you a good coach?

To paraphrase Tony Gummerson, 'How do you *know* you're a good coach?' Only when you have set objectives to achieve can you answer that.

Showing students how far they have improved is a valuable aid to maintaining enthusiasm and building self-confidence. The good coach does this by setting targets which students regard as difficult but not impossible to attain.

The student and coach must begin by defining exactly what the target is to be. Then they should prepare a plan to reach it. The plan will indicate where the target is in terms of time, financial cost, and availability of facilities and resources. The plan must be made so that progress can be measured and reinforced by support from team-mates, from the family, and from the coach.

The target must always be positive, stressing the need to do something rather than to avoid doing something. It must be perceived by the student as being within his control. For example, telling a student that he is to become an international champion is setting a target which includes elements over which he has no control. The target must be specific, so students know exactly what is called for. The coach must not say:

> 'I want you to kick higher.'

> Rather he should say:

> 'I want you to kick 2 inches higher.'

A date must be set by which the target must be achieved, because this focuses the mind and encourages application.

The coach shouldn't set too many targets too soon. Only one should be chosen at a time; when students become more experienced at relating to them, more targets can be introduced. It may well prove beneficial to identify lesser targets as necessary steps towards attaining the ultimate objective, and training priorities must be established by agreement between coach and students. Only those courses and events which conform to the training plan should be entered.

If students fail to reach the objectives, the coach must ask himself why. Did he set his sights too high within the time limit imposed? Did he select sensible targets? Did he select suitable students and train them in the right way? Is it someone else's fault (the get-out for the ineffective coach)? Is it the coach's own fault (this requires brutal self-analysis of coaching technique)? If the coach is strong enough to recognise his coaching shortcomings, then he is intelligent enough to do something about them.

Each training session must be planned so techniques are not unintentionally omitted. If necessary, the points to be covered can be written down on a piece of card and consulted throughout the session. However, a good coach will not plan to the exclusion of natural spontaneity. By this I mean that a particular class may get the bit between its teeth whilst doing a particular practice and when this happens it is often a good idea to allow it to continue a little longer than planned.

Communicating properly

The coach has to communicate with students in order to train them. Traditional martial arts instructors are authoritative in their approach to practice, so there is only a one-way flow of information. This is less effective than a two-way process. Feedback from students allows the coach to monitor more accurately the effect training is having on them.

The coach's appearance and demeanour are a form of non-verbal communication which provides information for the students to copy. If the coach comes late to training sessions, the students will, too. If the coach's training tunic is scruffy and unclean, the students will place no value on a good appearance. And so on.

How do students react to the coach's direction? If they don't respond as expected, did they understand what was said? Did the coach say what he thought he said? The coach causes confusion when he cannot clearly explain what he wants the students to do. I well remember my own early training under an oriental instructor whose total vocabulary consisted of 'More quickly!' and 'More hip-twist!' Anything that didn't fit either of those admonitions was either let pass or pointed out with a thump to the offending part.

After enough bruises, students discovered what they were doing wrong, though I wouldn't necessarily hold this up as an example of effective communication.

Often information is inappropriate to the standard of practice. The coach must give information according to the ability of the student. Too many details too soon will only confuse the novice.

Sometimes students don't listen. The good coach copes with this by gaining everyone's attention before he speaks, and then by making sure everyone can hear what is being said.

Experiments show that students register only 15%–20% of what is said to them. Therefore, the good coach tells them what they are to practise next; then he tells them what they are practising as they do it; and when they finish he tells them what they have just practised.

A coach with poor understanding of technique communicates his deficiencies to the students, so they perform techniques imperfectly. This is common in martial art associations which have undergone extensive splintering. If students lose faith in their coach's ability, they cease to regard his advice as useful, and communication breaks down.

If he talks too much they become bored and stop listening, so important information is missed. The good coach asks students why they think they didn't perform a technique correctly. This can yield very useful information. Coaches must talk *to* their students – not *down* to them!

A coach who does not know his students communicates with them in the wrong way. He may direct them to do things which they do not perceive as beneficial, or he may ruin their mental preparation by distracting them at the wrong time. He may try to psych them up and, in doing so, cause over-arousal, so they perform badly.

The good coach practises what he preaches. If, for example, he tells students that martial art is respectful and dignified, then yells and screams at referees during a tournament, his students will be confused and communication will suffer.

When coaches say they intend doing something, they must deliver! If a grading is scheduled, then it must take place: students are quick to pick up on broken promises.

Good coaching practice

The good coach uses sound judgement in the matter of technique progression and knows when a class is ready to be taught a particular technique. Many techniques rely upon earlier components which must be taught in the correct order; otherwise teaching the technique too early causes frustration when students cannot master it properly.

For example, perhaps the coach wishes to teach a roundhouse kick to the head. Few novices have the necessary degree of co-ordination and hip flexibility to perform this technique. When they inevitably fail, they say 'What's the use of training – I'm never going to be able to do this!' The good coach uses a technique progression, starting with a roundhouse kick to the body and gradually moving it upwards until the desired target is reached.

The lower target allows novices to achieve success and, bolstered by this, they are in the right frame of mind to tackle something a little more ambitious. Even if they fail, it is not a complete failure because they can always take one step back and achieve success again. Contrast this with novices who have nothing to fall back on. Theirs is a complete failure.

The good coach mixes body preparation training with technique progression, so the necessary components of physical fitness are on hand when it is time to practise a technique. Therefore, as novices work to a lower target with their roundhouse kicks, the coach introduces flexibility training so that when the time comes the necessary flexibility is available.

Technique progression is not cheating; neither is it a case of settling for second-best. What is the use of a high roundhouse kick which is poorly performed? It is far better to encourage novices to perform skilful techniques to a lower height, because this allows technique form to develop properly.

During intensive practice of jumping kicks, the occasional hard landing is the rule rather than the exception. This causes pain, if not injury, and, if steps are not taken to remove anxiety, the technique may become degraded. Therefore, the good coach allays anxiety by providing a safe landing. Some of the best jumping kicks I have seen performed by novices happened when they were larking about in a swimming bath. In all cases, the exhibitors vanished in a painless cloud of spray! I'm not, of course, suggesting that you transform your training hall into a swimming pool! Enough soft mats will suffice.

The good coach analyses all the techniques in the syllabus and, where the class experiences obvious difficulty, he makes modifications which remove the problem without abandoning the technique's integrity. This is creative coaching. There is still lee-way for fruitful experimentation even when following a rigid syllabus.

Free sparring is an area where good coaching may conflict with expediency. In those martial arts where it is practised, there is a great pressure from novices to participate. Yet it is a fact that more injuries occur during free sparring than in any other aspect of practice. This risk decreases as the participants' skill increases, so it is a matter of good coaching practice to introduce free sparring only when students have reached a suitable standard in their basic skills.

Most martial art classes contain above 20 students, which means that the coach's ministrations are spread thinly. Nevertheless, it is still possible to apply good coaching practice. To cope with such classes, the good coach must know the students, recognising that some learn at different rates. Slower learners require longer to master a technique than others, so if he wants to keep them, he mustn't skip too quickly to the next technique! Spare time is used to go into greater detail with those who have already mastered the essentials. The coach never begins each session with new techniques. He starts, instead, with a résumé of the previous lesson before passing on to something new.

Coaching for personal excellence

Some coaches are naturally better than others at handling a large class. They develop a 'feel' for the class's collective attitude and direct it so that enthusiasm is generated and everyone finishes on a higher level than when they started. Each individual martial artist receives less personal attention than he would in a smaller class, but this does not stop the good coach from knowing the performance and needs of each student.

Other coaches work best with a smaller number of highly motivated students.

In both cases the coach must have the correct physical abilities, enough experience, the right attitude and, above all, he must be available in the right place at the right time. The good coach contributes as much as 60% towards students' success. The remaining 40% is up to the students themselves.

Everyone, including physically and mentally disadvantaged people, is capable of achieving personal excellence. The aim of good coaching is to help all students attain it.

The training hall must be right for developing excellence. It must be accessible so students need not spend a long time travelling to reach it. It must also be readily available so that training sessions can be held as often as required. It should have a good atmosphere, a comfortable temperature and all the necessary facilities to allow students and coach to concentrate on training. Ancillary equipment, such as weights, must be on hand.

Students pushing themselves to the limit soon develop aches and strains and there is much to be said for the ministrations of a physiotherapist!

In pursuit of personal excellence, even the training time must be right. Did you know that the body reaches its peak between 2.00 and 4.00 p.m. each day? Eating a heavy dinner after a hard day's work and then setting off for intensive training during the evening is not the most effective way to train for a personal best.

Training camps are very good for achieving improvements. People far enough away from their everyday environment are better able to concentrate on training. For greatest benefit, the camp must be convivial and preferably set in a warm climate. Students who desperately want to improve must give enough time to training, if necessary to the exclusion of other aspects of private and family life.

Talent spotting

To discover the ideal mix of physical and mental characteristics in a martial art, the coach makes a list of all the best exponents in the different age groups and sees what they have in common. He may be able to pick out common characteristics which he can then look for amongst his students. These will tell the coach what chance the 60 kilo, 5 feet tall 30-year-old novice has of achieving his declared aim of becoming world openweight karate champion.

The coach looks for such things as the range of flexibility in key joints, such as the hip and shoulder. He looks, too, for powerful muscles, co-ordination and agility. He should ask himself the following questions:

- are the student's body proportions correct for the martial art?
- are his legs the right length in relation to his body?
- has the student good reach?
- is the student highly competitive, and able to put on a top performance under the stress of a grading or competition?

The coach talent spots by encouraging participation in the club through well publicised 'Come and try it' days. He encourages students to keep training because talent does not always show up early in the training programme. Even if the coach doesn't find talent, he will nevertheless be promoting the club and generating a positive attitude towards martial art practice.

Coaching children and young people

More and more young people are taking to martial art practice, and the coach must become aware of the differences which distinguish them from adult students. Children grow in fits and starts, so don't be surprised if the young chap you've been training to enter the under-5-feet-tall Boys' Competition measures in on the day at 5 feet 1 inch!

The young girl who showed so much promise at the age of 11 may taper off 2 years later. Is it perhaps because she was a precocious performer who has now 'shot her bolt'? Coach everyone – not just current achievers. Youngsters mature at different rates and the undistinguished spotty lad in the back row may suddenly turn out to be a late developer.

Children and young people love to train, not to listen to longwinded instructions. Bear this in mind if you want to keep them in membership.

Allow children to take part in most aspects of club training, but always be aware of their physical limitations and emotional immaturity. Many children love to compete, so make up safe competitions for them, preferably of the type where everyone wins something or other.

The wider context of coaching

It is often claimed that coaches are not interested in martial art politics. When all is going well, they need not be, but when there is competition for training halls or grant aid, an astute coach can get his case to the front of the queue.

Good coaches are effective politicians anyway because they deal in human relation-ships, balancing one ego against another. I have sat in the offices of one national coach, listening with growing admiration at the way he handled inter-club disputes and bad student/club coach interactions. This man not only knows his coaches but he also has a knowledge of practical psychology and a political approach to keep everyone pulling together.

It is no bad thing if the coach knows a little about the Law. The tendency nowadays is to settle disputes of all kinds through the courts. The problem is that the coach may not realise the extent of his duty, or the nature of the Law which governs it. Martial art coaches are being sued in Britain today and there is no reason to think this trend will diminish. Therefore, the coach owes it to himself (and to his family) to find out what his legal liabilities are, and then to work within known confines.

The good coach is a credible person. He is sensible in that if he runs one small club in Ecclefechan, he doesn't refer to it as 'British' or 'International'. Similarly, he doesn't make himself look silly by claiming pretentious titles. 'Master', 'Grand Master' and 'Professor' are titles reserved for top coaches with international reputations.

Whenever he advertises his club, he always identifies it properly and avoids confusing initials. He never makes bold claims, such as saying that his club is the 'biggest and best in Britain' unless he knows for a fact that it is. If he runs a little competition between his club and one belonging to a pen-pal in Malaga, he doesn't publicise it as 'England v Spain'.

His club operates according to a set of rules, copies of which are available to the membership.

The coach may need to acquire and spend money effectively. Mats have to be provided and/or a certain amount of kit made available for newcomers. It is not a good idea to rely upon the charity of sports councils and local authorities; funds must be raised both directly from the membership and indirectly through the club's activities. This all requires a certain flair for organisation.

The coach must clearly understand how he fits into the martial art scheme of things, if only to relate to sources of information and advice. Appendix 1 sets out how the martial arts in Britain are organised.

Let me leave you with a cautionary tale. A high grade martial artist of my past acquaintance claimed to be unemployed whilst he was, in fact, running a large and prosperous club. One night a man came along and asked to join. On payment of the fee, he was admitted and began training. He asked the usual questions that beginners always ask, such as 'How many people belong to this club? How often does it train? How long has it been going?'

After a couple of weeks the man dropped out and was never seen again. However, about a month after that, two officials called on the instructor and presented him with a very large bill for back Inland Revenue.

With that very much in mind, let's now summarise this chapter by listing the requirements for a good coach.

He must:

- be a highly skilled martial artist with a deep knowledge of the martial art and its syllabus
- have a good knowledge of other martial arts
- have been through the same training that the students face and be acknowledged by them as leader
- have a positive outlook on training
- know the students, their hopes and aspirations
- show loyalty to the students and always act in their best interests
- be flexible in approach
- have a secure and enlightened ego
- set coaching objectives and monitor progress towards their attainment
- teach good techniques at the correct time, in the correct order and in a manner which accommodates different aptitude levels
- be an innovator of technique and teaching method
- be a credible person, a good politician, a training-hall lawyer and a sound business person.

Seeing the principles of coaching actually working in your training hall will encourage you to seek more knowledge. Refer to pages 182–3 to find out where you fit into the MAC Coaching Award Scheme.

Questions

Discover how much of this last chapter you have absorbed by answering the following questions.

1 Do you consider that you know enough about your martial art to be able to teach it to others?
2 Do you know the full history of your martial art?
3 Do you know anything about other martial arts?
4 At what grade should someone be eligible to become a coach?
5 Give an example of how insensitive coaching can drive away promising students.
6 The coach's main obligation is to whom?
7 Name two cornerstones upon which coach/student relationships are built.
8 Give reasons why splintering occurs and suggest ways of dealing with it.
9 Are you aware of any deficiencies in your technique?
10 What are your objectives in coaching?
11 How will you assess your coaching ability?
12 What benefits will your coaching bring to students, apart from improving their technical ability?
13 How do you set your targets?
14 What form should targets take?
15 Describe the elements which make up good communication.
16 What is technique progression?
17 What does 'personal best' mean?
18 What is the best time of day to train?
19 How do you recognise talent in your club?
20 How do martial art politics help you to keep your club thriving?
21 What should you avoid when promoting yourself and your club?
22 List the requirements for a good coach.

PRACTICAL COACHING

Gaining attention

Move to a particular spot from which to call the class to attention. Position yourself so you can be easily seen and clap your hands to gain attention. Always use the same spot and the same method for gaining attention.

Thank the students for their attention.

If someone is not paying attention, move closer and address him by name whilst asking for attention. Do not lose your cool and, if he still does not co-operate, speak privately to him at a later stage during training.

Appear enthusiastic, avoiding sarcasm, abusive language and annoying habits, such as repeating words like 'You know...'

Plan what you are going to say before you open your mouth. Speak clearly, firmly and politely, using a slightly louder voice than you normally use for conversation. Aim to be heard by the most distant member of the class and do not shout or become shrill.

Adapt your manner of speech to suit the class. Speak simply and avoid jargon which the class may not understand.

Be brief!

Vary inflection and tone so your voice becomes interesting to listen to and not a dreary monotonous drone. Reinforce what you are saying by making eye contact with members of the class.

Make sure everyone can see you clearly whilst you are speaking. If students are milling around, leaning on walls or standing on tiptoe, you won't be able to hold their attention. Arrange them in a semicircle, with yourself as the focal point and, if necessary, have the front row sit down cross-legged.

It is always a good idea to ask children to sit down.

If you are training in a multi-user sports hall, ensure nothing is happening behind you to distract students' attention. If you train out of doors, don't face students into the sun.

When people begin fidgeting or looking around, that is a clear sign that you have gone on for too long.

Demonstrating the technique

Clearly name the technique you are going to demonstrate and if the reason for using it is not immediately clear, give a brief description of why it is used.

Explain that it will be demonstrated first in full flight, then it will be slowed down and perhaps interrupted to pick out salient points.

Consider selecting a competent member of the class or an assistant coach to demonstrate the technique. I have seen coaches try to explain how to escape from a stranglehold as it is being applied to them, and sounding like Mickey Mouse in the process!

Repeat the technique from different angles and, if appropriate, show it both in right-handed and left-handed forms. Point out the various features, but do not go into too much detail.

Try to relate the technique being demonstrated to an action with which students will be familiar. One leading British karate instructor used to explain the mechanism of the reverse punch by likening it to throwing a ball. I found this very effective in explaining an otherwise complex movement to total novices.

Ask for questions, repeating them for the benefit of the rest of the class. Make your answers brief and related specifically to the technique being demonstrated.

Let the class begin practising immediately after the demonstration, but ensure they are properly spread out and away from areas of potential hazard.

Distribute more senior students throughout the class so their practice can be used as an example for the novices.

If you have presented the technique in an effective manner, the class will work hard at it. If they don't, ask them why they are not doing so. Perhaps they are frightened of hurting each other. In that case, show how the technique can be controlled. If they find the technique boring, re-examine your whole coaching approach.

If most of the class are doing the technique incorrectly, stop the students and demonstrate it again.

If you are performing a kata/poomse/pattern, go through the movements with the class, but face in the same direction as the students are, so they can more easily relate to which arm and leg you are moving, and in what direction. Check by looking over your shoulder that everyone is performing the techniques with you.

If you tackle a long sequence and students become confused, break it down into a series of sections, identifying these by numbers, or by key words which sum up what is being done at that point. When the class can perform each separate component correctly, string all the bits together to complete the sequence and thereafter always coach it as a whole movement.

You may find that a common mistake crops up. If so, stop the class and demonstrate the mistake, say why it is wrong and then perform the correct technique. If difficulty persists, ask assistant coaches or students what the problem is and use this information to modify your approach.

Interrupt the class as little as possible. Keep everyone active and let them finish what they are doing before you stop them.

After general errors have been dealt with, begin spending time on individual students but don't spend all your time with talented performers.

Watch how students perform techniques, then explain simply and concisely what they have done wrong by comparing it with what should be done. Make sure the student understands what you have said and then encourage further practice.

Analyse errors to see whether one is causing the others. Correct a basic fault and the technique will show an immediate improvement.

If errors are unrelated, select the most serious and correct that. This will lead to an improvement in technique which motivates the student to eliminate the other errors. Do not draw the student's attention to more than one error at a time.

Motivate students by praising parts of the technique which are correct – but avoid giving insincere or false praise.

Partner practice is useful for providing corrective feedback. One performs a technique and the other responds to it. After a while, the passive partner becomes able to identify and point out basic errors, such as timing, distance and line.

While everyone is practising, select a small group of students and show them the next technique to be practised. When they are doing it correctly, clap your hands to stop the class and tell everyone to look on as the new technique is performed.

Working to a plan

The following is a practical example of how to prepare Jack to turn in a personal best performance during his black belt grading.

Jack is eligible to take this grading in 12 months' time, so how will the coach ensure that he arrives on the day in the peak of physical and mental condition? This is done by means of 'peaking'. Experiments have shown that it is possible to peak only twice in a year, though several additional lower peaks can be attained!

Jack has just taken his last grading before black belt and is enjoying a well deserved rest. During this time he is recovering from injuries whilst maintaining a basic level of aerobic fitness by running, cycling or swimming. He performs no martial art techniques as such. This rest period is followed by a period of light training as he begins once more to take up the load. Techniques must be practised and new ones learned. Flexibility training resumes and old injury sites are strengthened.

As time goes by, the pace of training accelerates. The new syllabus requirements have been learned and are being practised under conditions of steadily increasing power and flexibility. Additional fitness sessions make good specific shortcomings in flexibility whilst increasing anaerobic endurance to cope with training load.

As the date for grading approaches, more and more emphasis is placed on technique performance and skill. Jack is now training to perform over the same time and in the same manner as he will in the grading itself. Periods of maximum effort are interspersed with long recovery intervals. Finally, during the last couple of days, training intensity drops sharply, so Jack wakes up on the day feeling rested, fit and confident.

THE RELATIONSHIP OF COACHING TO SKILL

What is skill?

A skilful martial artist consistently selects appropriate actions and techniques, and performs them to a high standard. Used in the context of sparring, for example, 'skill' means selecting exactly the right techniques and approach to achieve a successful outcome. The skilled martial artist has a 'low technique redundancy rate' and almost every technique employed actually succeeds. Compare this with the unskilled novice who fires off techniques like bullets from a machine gun in the hope that one will find a target.

The skilled martial artist knows exactly what he is trying to achieve, the most effective way of achieving it, and the most efficient usage of effort.

The skilled person has trained for many years and has gained a great amount of experience upon which he can draw. Experience helps skill because:

- the person remembers previous similar circumstances and how they developed
- the person recalls what previously worked (and didn't work) in those circumstances.

Without experience, martial artists must face each situation as it arises, and must make the best of it.

Skills are learned efficiently when students enjoy practising and it always helps if they can see the point in doing something. Less efficient is learning under threat of disapproval from the coach, parents, or peer group. Also less efficient is learning simply to achieve an external target as, for example, being able to beat everybody up! What happens when such a student meets (as he surely will) someone larger and tougher?

To promote efficient learning the coach must:

- select forms of practice appropriate to the class's interest, requirements and capability
- provide some means whereby students can see that they are improving through training
- stress all aspects of martial art practice, not merely those of winning competitions, or achieving 1st class gradings.

Learning occurs most efficiently in short and intense training sessions, rather than in drawn-out and leisurely ones. Practice should be varied both to maintain interest and to work all parts of the body.

Smaller syllabuses are learned more quickly than larger ones and lead to early and accurate reproductions of movements and techniques. Larger syllabuses take longer but give rise to greater adaptability.

The learning process is helped when students rehearse techniques, sequences and tactics in their heads prior to using them. This, of course, can only be done if they have previous experience to work on. The karate student must know a kata before he can rehearse it in his head. As he does rehearse it, his brain works exactly as it would were he actually performing the kata but with one exception: the link to the motor system is switched off, so he doesn't sit there twitching spasmodically!

Unfortunately, it isn't possible to train all the way to black belt by mental rehearsal alone and there is no substitute for training. The more often students physically perform a technique, the less likely they are to forget it.

The coach helps learning by providing less experienced students with feedback on what they are doing wrong and with advice on how to correct their errors. By comparison, more experienced students perform techniques automatically and monitor their execution by reference to whether or not they feel right. Small adjustments are overlaid on the basic technique performance to adjust it for factors such as changing distance. Lots of changing information is selectively 'read' and the necessary corrections are made. Under these circumstances, the coach's advice confirms what an experienced student already knows.

The coach watches a number of performances before picking up on uncorrected errors. Correction must follow shortly after the performance, but not so soon that the student has no time to switch from self-assessment to external assessment.

Mirrors provide useful feedback because they allow students to examine their own techniques. Kinaesthetic awareness is knowing where one part of the body is in relation to another. For example, novices might be performing a kata/poomse/pattern and the coach tells them to raise their hands to the same level during a block. Because most people can't pinpoint the position of an arm (or a leg) without looking at it, the arms will be at different heights.

Items of equipment can also be used. For example, a chair back provides a good incentive for aligning the hip, knee and ankle during a roundhouse kick (*see photograph 1*). A lightweight plastic pole can be used to show the correct position of the upper body during the same kick (*see photograph 2*). Through this feedback, the student comes to learn kinaesthetic awareness, so when the coach asks for a specific action to be performed, then it is duly executed with precision!

It is always best to practise techniques as whole movements, rather than breaking them up into smaller ones. When martial arts became popular, the requirements of large classes encouraged coaches to chop complex movements into serialised steps. By this means, students might learn first to block a technique and then to counter-attack. By comparison, in smaller traditional schools of martial art, the

1. Using a chair to help get correct leg/foot alignment during a roundhouse kick

2. Using a plastic pole as a training aid to show correct upper body position during a roundhouse kick

attack was integrated seamlessly into the defence, making it more effective.

Many problems in learning occur because students cannot relate what they are doing to what is being asked for! There is a lack of spatial awareness, of kinaesthetic awareness, or of both. Spatial awareness is knowing the position of the body in relation to the floor or to a target.

For example, the taekwondo practitioner performing a jumping, reverse wheel kick must produce a whole series of movements in the air, culminating in an accurate kick to a small target area. This requires spatial awareness because if synchronisation and movement are not correlated, the kick goes all over the place – if it is delivered at all! Spatial awareness is developed through technique progression.

To learn is to progress, to create and to invent. The student who is locked into a rigid syllabus, practising the same techniques over and over again eventually reaches a learning 'ceiling'. The only improvement thereafter is an imperceptible rise in technique proficiency.

Learning theories

The coach can detect improvement in skill level as students train and this tells him that they are learning. The rate at which they learn will depend, amongst other things, on their powers of concentration, on their ability at mentally reviewing and rehearsing what the coach has said, and on their ability to interpret internal and external feedback.

No one knows quite how the process of learning works and various hypotheses named 'Learning Theories' have been devised to explain it. 'Rote Learning' postulates that any skill can be learned through continual repetition. It is the chief method used in martial art classes but suffers from the disadvantage that too much serial repetition leads to boredom.

'Imitation Learning' is used with Rote Learning to teach the martial arts. It works on the basis that a less skilled person imitates the action of more skilled participants. It is, of course, essential that the technique to be taught is performed both correctly and always in the same way.

The instructors where I trained all taught slight variations of technique and it was a headache trying to remember which instructor favoured which variation!

'Classical Pavlovian Conditioning' postulates that techniques can be learned in such a way as to set up a conditioned reflex. Conditioned reflexes need no conscious thought and the techniques they generate are therefore performed more quickly.

'Trial and Error' learning is a way of assessing techniques by measuring their effectiveness under practical circumstances. Some techniques work whilst others apparently do not. The former are kept and the latter are discarded. No doubt this was the system adopted in the battlefield; the successful technique guaranteed victory, the less effective technique . . .

'Project' learning is sometimes used to train more advanced students. They are asked to respond to a situation by originating technique combinations and practical responses. Trial and Error learning takes place after origination and those which work are kept, whilst those which do not are discarded.

'Transfer of Training' particularly interests me. It postulates that basic and applied techniques should be as similar as possible. If, for example, I practise a basic reverse punch which leaves my arm locked out, the skill I develop cannot be easily transferred to a reverse punch in which the punching arm is quickly retrieved after use. The Transfer of Learning theory recommends me to practise my reverse punch in exactly the manner I will apply it.

'Operant Conditioning' learning theory uses a reward to encourage learning. The reward may be a few words of praise, for this has a better effect than a hundred words of criticism. Judiciously used, praise creates a need to earn more praise, so increasing motivation.

Learning does not continue at the same rate throughout a student's training career. It is highest at the beginning, perhaps because new students are very enthusiastic and learn the easy bits first, adapting non-martial art skills to help them.

This rapid rate of learning soon levels off and though students continue to train hard, they seem to make no real progress. If left unresolved, this brings about disillusionment. The good coach combats it by changing to another form of practice, or by removing the weakness causing the training block. By comparison, the unskilled coach keeps going along in the same old rut and class numbers begin to fall.

When the training blockage is passed, learning once more accelerates, but this time neither for so long a period nor so quickly as in the first instance. Eventually a second and longer 'no progress plateau' is reached. The cycle repeats and, as time goes by, the periods of learning steadily reduce in relation to intervals of no progress.

The good coach monitors rate of improvement and when it eases, he knows the reason for it. For example, a competitive squad may reach a peak and go no further. The good coach realises that they now need a new challenge, such as an actual competition. The artless coach simply goes on to overtrain them. This leads to a breakdown in performance, characterised by loss of skill, build-up of frustration and deterioration in health.

Frustration occurs when a martial artist is not achieving what he feels he could, or not doing what he feels he ought. Sometimes it comes about because the coach is pushing him in a direction he does not want to go. For example, the person who enrolled to learn self defence may not be interested in competition, despite his obvious talents for it. In this case the coach must decide whether to lose the student altogether by forcing him into competition, or to drop him from the squad but otherwise keep him in membership.

Students are all individuals and respond to the coach's direction in their own individual ways. Some have stronger legs, others are more flexible; some are 'laid-back', others are competitive. The coach must recognise this individuality and must train them accordingly. The poor coach tries to turn out models of himself.

The essence of good coaching is that all students must be made to feel they are improving by reference to their own abilities. They do not fail simply because they cannot match the over-achievers in the class.

Motivating students to perform better

Motivation depends upon the martial artist's personality and what he expects to get out of training. Nearly every novice wants to become an expert, but soon realises the degree of commitment and effort needed. Many young martial artists train because their parents want them to. They are encouraged to chase after grades, and drop out once they reach black belt. Such students drop out even faster when they don't get the next grading, or they fail to place in the championships. An over-emphasis on succeeding at gradings, or on winning competitions, can reduce motivation because students will come to see training only as a means to an end. Training becomes single-minded and much natural enjoyment is lost. Eventually, not even an extra large gold medal or a new and flashy certificate will replace lost motivation. With nothing else going for them, such students give up practice altogether.

Some students settle down and train steadily from grading to grading, without ever achieving or wanting to achieve personal excellence.

On the surface, it seems that Fred isn't interested in winning, yet he works very hard and enjoys training. Fred actually has an internal motivation to satisfy. Training makes him feel rewarded because within his frame of values, martial art practice has a high priority.

Strongly motivated students succeed regardless of whether they are technically proficient or fit enough. By comparison, talented performers are often the least motivated and are amongst the first to drop out when the going gets tough. From the coach's point of view, a class of average triers is more rewarding than one of laconic over-achievers.

There comes a time when even the most highly motivated martial artists become bored with practice. The good coach combats this by varying training from lesson to lesson. He makes sure that no one knows exactly what they will be doing before they arrive.

When there is a good relationship between coach and student, the coach's praise increases motivation. Even errors pointed out in a helpful and positive manner improve it. Compare two sets of advice to Jill. The first is:

■ 'Your hip throw is diabolical!'

The second is:

■ 'You've made some good progress but there is still a problem with that hip throw. You're just not getting your centre of gravity under Jane's.'

The second advice praises Jill's progress and then identifies a correctable error. Verbal rewards must be informational. Let students know what they are doing well and stress all the advantages of martial art practice, not just winning. The good coach gives rewards for effort – not just for success.

The coach and students must develop a good training relationship, free from all resentment and problems. Both coach and martial artist must be able to accept criticism without rancour.

The bad coach inflicts body preparation on students as though it is a form of punishment. This makes them see preparation work as something they are obliged to do, rather than something they want to do. By way of contrast, gymnastics needs good body preparation and B.A.G.A. National Coach John White trains it into children by using games.

For example, to improve strength in back muscles, he doesn't make them perform plain hyper-extensions. Instead, they play 'Superman', lying on their tummies and pretending to fly by arching their backs. Because the exercise is seen as a game, the children are motivated to work much harder at it.

Resilience must be built into motivation to help students overcome physical and mental setbacks. It comes from within and can be increased by a word of praise, or a burst of cheering. Resilience pulls martial artists out of those depressions which afflict so many at different times in their training careers.

Motivation must include a measure of aggression, but having said that, the coach must be on the look-out to ensure students don't go over the top!

Questions
1 What is meant by the term 'skill'?
2 How can experience help responses?
3 How may skills be most quickly learned?
4 How does mental rehearsal work?
5 Suggest ways of providing feedback using equipment.
6 How should verbal feedback be given?
7 List the various learning theories.
8 How does the coach deal with students' frustration?
9 What are the disadvantages of basing motivation on winning tournaments?
10 How does the coach deal with periods of no progress?
11 Describe ways of making exercises more interesting.
12 What is the meaning of the term 'resilience'?
13 Is aggression a useful emotion for students?

THE PRINCIPLES OF FITNESS

Fitness and practice

The purpose of martial art practice is to progress in knowledge and technique. This comes about in three ways, the first being progression in understanding the art, the second being progression in the improvement of technique and the third being progression in mental and physical fitness. It is with the last progression that this chapter concerns itself.

If I had a penny for every student who came to see me and asked how to improve hip flexibility, I'd now be a rich man. All martial art coaches must know about human physiology (the way the body works) if they are to train students effectively. If armed with this knowledge, they both understand how training affects the body and why some forms of training are more beneficial than others. Without this knowledge, they are labouring in the dark. At the conclusion of this chapter, I have listed some of the training faults currently to be found in the average martial art club.

A martial art requires both a certain level and type of fitness so students can acquire skill quickly through being able to:

a   train hard through the session without running out of breath
b   reach and maintain the required levels of power delivery in kicks, strikes and throws
c   move with sufficient co-ordination, balance and agility to apply martial art techniques
d   respond quickly and correctly to attacks, feints and openings
e   reach the required degree of flexibility to perform techniques correctly and safely.

Surprisingly, martial art training alone is unlikely to provide either the level or type of fitness required, unless of course you practise 8 hours a day and 5 + days a week. Assuming this is impossible, supplementary fitness training is essential. There are two views in relation to fitness training and martial art practice. One is that students do not pay money to perform press-ups; they pay to learn martial art technique, so fitness considerations are a matter for the individual student. Where training sessions are short and classes large, this view has merit. The second view holds that the martial art coach is responsible for teaching all those factors which, taken together, will allow the student to master the techniques studied. This must obviously include the required level of fitness.

I tend to take the middle line and consider that all classes should contain a certain amount of fitness training, with students encouraged also to train outside the training hall. Whichever view you take, I'm sure you will agree that when two martial artists of equal technical ability face each other, the one who is fitter has an advantage.

Systematic and progressive training is related to fitness levels such that:

a   infrequent training will not improve fitness level; the body only responds to physical demands made frequently; therefore train regularly and often

b   lazy training will not improve the fitness level. The tissues of the body must be subjected to controlled stress if a training effect is to occur; therefore train hard

c   training too hard early on in the programme may result in injury; start gently and gradually increase the pace of training so the body has time to respond to the new demands placed on it

d   training for the wrong fitness factors develops fitness which is unrelated to that needed for your martial art; lots of road work, for example, will produce marathon runners rather than martial artists!

e   when training stops, fitness levels decline; the fine edge of timing is the first casualty, and this is quickly followed by a drop in skill; speed is next lost, followed by endurance and strength

f   training too hard for too long is not beneficial; over-worked students are prone to injury and lose motivation; therefore, alternate hard sessions with lighter ones.

The coach must have a clear understanding of each of these principles, so training can be properly programmed to yield maximum benefit.

A working definition of fitness

We've talked a bit about fitness, but what exactly is it? Fitness is a state of being in which various factors work together to equip the body for what it is doing. I will go into more detail about the way martial art training affects the body in the next chapter, but for now let's list these factors and refer to them generally:

a   *Aerobic endurance:* this is the ability of heart, lungs and circulation to transport oxygen and food to working muscles, and at the same time efficiently to remove waste matter. When the muscles are working comparatively lightly – even over a long period – they can make good use of oxygen brought by the blood. Aerobic endurance is a good base upon which to build other aspects of fitness. Aerobic training aims to improve the efficiency of the heart, lungs and circulation.

b   *Anaerobic endurance:* this is the ability of the muscles to continue working both without oxygen and with a build-up of waste materials. Each muscle contains reserves of energy which are used up during the first few contractions in a process that does not require oxygen. Later, when the training session becomes more intense and the muscles work harder, the blood is unable to furnish as much oxygen as is required and so the muscles have to switch to an alternative system which can work without it. Unfortunately, this results in the build-up of a waste product called **lactic acid** which clogs muscle action. If anaerobic endurance is taken to its limit, muscles become exhausted and lose the power to contract. Anaerobic training builds tolerance to high lactic acid levels.

c   *Local endurance:* this is the ability of a local group of muscles to continue working effectively. For example, sit-ups test the endurance of the abdominal muscles only. The coach needs to identify those muscles which are most heavily worked during training and then to select exercises which will extend their endurance.

d   *Strength:* this is the maximum force a muscle, or group of muscles, can exert in one contraction. Strong muscles are important for holding joints together. There are basically three types of strength, the first being **isometric**, the second being **isotonic** and the third named **isokinetic**. Isometric strength can be developed through stance work, or through apparatus such as the 'Bullworker'. Isotonic strength improves with body weight exercises and by using external weights. Isokinetic strength matches the speed of contraction of a muscle with a varying load, but training for this requires expensive equipment.

e   *Speed:* this is the rate of contraction of a muscle or group of muscles. The speed at which a muscle contracts is related to the type of fibres it contains. Muscles which contain a high proportion of white fibres contract more quickly than those which contain mainly red fibres. By practising techniques repeatedly, an overall increase in speed of execution will develop as skill level and understanding increase.

f   *Reaction:* this is the time that passes between the recognition of a cue and the response to it. The incoming technique is first seen and is then identified. Correct identification is followed by selection of a suitable response technique from the options available, and then by the physical execution of the response. Many factors play a part in producing a fast reaction. Included amongst these are an advance knowledge of the opponent's favourite techniques, a recognition of any patterns of technique usage which might occur and a pre-selection of the response to be used (where this is appropriate). One of the most important factors is the martial artist's skill level. The less involvement conscious mental processes play in the process, the faster a technique can be executed.

g   *Power:* this is a combination of strength and the speed at which a muscle, or group of muscles, can contract. From the martial artist's point of view, power is more important than strength. If you think about it, there is an obvious link between power and local muscular endurance. Training for power involves practising techniques (or exercises based on those techniques) with a light loading on the muscles. The techniques/exercises must be performed at high speed.

h *Suppleness:* this is the range of movement at a joint, or series of joints. Joints are closely associated with muscles which must be stretched if a student with low flexibility is to improve. The training programme progressively stretches the relaxed muscle by means of body weight, or with added pressure from a trusted partner.

i *Agility:* this is a combination of factors, such as reaction, speed, strength and co-ordination. Agility can be improved by training with suitable traditional training patterns (**Kata**, **Poomse**, etc.), or by using exercises.

j *Body composition:* this is the percentage of lean to fat tissue in the body. Unless you are a Sumo wrestler, the benefits of excess fat (i.e. increased mass, momentum and the cushioning of hard blows) will be outweighed by the disadvantages. Reduce fat tissue by a combination of correct nutrition and increased training.

k *Motivation:* this is the determination the student has to endure training in order to reach a particular goal. A student with low motivation will not endure the hardships necessary to reach a high standard of practice. Good coaching will improve motivation by demonstrating a continuing improvement, or by counselling a student over a setback or training block.

In addition to the above, age, sex and heredity play important roles in terms of maximum performance. There is a gradual decline in physical ability with advancing age. This is ultimately irreversible, though the degenerative process can be held back through regular training. Improved technique can do much to off-set the decline in power and flexibility and though there might be no 70-year-old world champions, there are many 70-year-old masters of martial art.

Two major factors appear to affect the participation of males and females in the martial arts. The first is 'intrinsic' (coming from within) and is related to the production of the male hormone **testosterone**. This seems to stimulate aggression. The second factor is 'extrinsic' (coming from outside) and comes about through the way male and female children are brought up. Boys typically fight and play at combat sports, whereas girls do not. This is probably why female martial artists pitted against males of similar mass and experience generally lose.

Our physical and perhaps mental make-up are derived from our parents' separate ancestries and if we inherit a short, slight frame and muscles which contain a preponderance of red fibres, we are clearly unlikely to become open-weight world champions. This is the effect our heredity has on our potential. We can certainly improve power, suppleness and reaction times through training, though when we face opponents who are trained to the same degree *and*, in addition, are 2 metres tall with commensurate reach, we remain at a disadvantage.

Specificity of fitness

We briefly mentioned this topic earlier in the section. The relationship of the various fitness factors to each other will determine the type of fitness developed. The fitness requirements for different forms of practice within the same martial art may vary, so let's consider the requirements for three different aspects of training – the training itself, the grading and the competition.

During the basic training session the class practises a sequence of moves over and over again, either in lines or in pairs (or both). This activity is typically not performed with maximum power because all present know they have to train for a full two hours. Accordingly, the overall workload is lower, though certain muscles will be used more than others. Very soon the latter begin to feel fatigued as lactic acid builds up in them, yet the rest of the body is relatively unstressed. The working limbs operate through a range of movement which requires a certain amount of flexibility.

The clever coach then switches to a second sequence which perhaps involves other muscle groups, allowing the first set to get rid of the lactic acid they have built up. This sequence, too, is performed at less than maximum power. The heart rate may have increased somewhat and the lungs are pumping air in greater volumes. Other joints are now being worked through their full range of movement.

As the training session progresses towards its half-way point, an increased rate of work may be called for. The good coach knows when this can be brought on because he is feeling the mood of the class. The students step up technique usage, so muscle fatigue comes on more quickly, and when the class is just reaching its peak, the coach calls a halt and quickly changes the practice again.

A proper rest is not given because the pumping muscles must be encouraged to get rid of the waste materials produced through training. An 'active' rest consisting of less demanding work is given instead and, when the coach feels the class has benefited, training once more accelerates.

Kata/Poomse/pattern practice occupies a large segment of most training sessions. On the skill side, this teaches familiarity with modular technique application in a way that other training does not. For example, combination techniques may link three or four moves together into (usually) a linear series, whereas pattern practice links sometimes more than a hundred in broken, non-linear series. The result of this is to help the student perform linked techniques without conscious intervention, therefore making them faster.

On the fitness side, pattern practice builds whole body and local muscular endurance. It also promotes agility, maintains flexibility in skilled martial artists, and the stances improve isometric strength in the muscles concerned.

The session may well conclude with free, or semi-free, sparring when students exchange unprogrammed techniques for anything up to 20 minutes. This sparring consists of periods of low activity interspersed with brief flurries of more demanding work.

Would you say this was a fair summary of what you do in your club? If yes, then apart from skill, your students will need:

- the ability to keep going at less than maximum pace for the whole of the session, i.e. **aerobic** endurance
- the ability for some groups of muscles to perform harder than others over a prolonged period, so they become fatigued; this is **local** muscular endurance. Identify the muscles used by observing the techniques
- the ability to move the whole body and limbs quickly, and to change direction suddenly and without warning (**agility** and **speed**)
- the ability to move all the joints through the desired range of movement, both generally in the body and with specific application to certain joints, such as the hip (**flexibility**)
- the ability to apply sufficient strength to make a technique succeed
- the ability to react in sufficient time to the opponent's actions.

All of these fitness requirements are inter-related and if the training session I have described does not match yours, then sit down and do your own analysis!

Compare this now with the grading examination. A number of students who have prepared for this day are brought to their feet and put through a part of the syllabus. For up to 5 minutes they will work at near their maximum rate on a repetition basis. Cessation of activity is sudden, and when their turn is over they will sit down and may not be called again for a long period. The good coach will ensure that the finished students go to a different area of the training hall and cool down.

When the first group of students are called up again they perform a second set of techniques. Some clubs require a whole series of patterns to be performed, one after the other and with a rest of perhaps only 30 seconds between each. Patterns use relatively few repetitions.

The final stage of the grading may require a series of free sparring bouts, where activity peaks are more frequent and powerful than in normal class sparring. There is little repetition. In one school of martial art, the examinee may have to fight up to 100 people successively.

If this is a fair summary of how you conduct your gradings (less the 100 person line-up perhaps!), then apart from skill, your students will require:

- the correct preparation for the grading
- the ability to work at near maximum effort for a period of perhaps 5 or so minutes (**anaerobic** endurance)
- the ability to perform techniques at a high speed for the duration of the interval
- the flexibility to perform techniques
- the ability to react quickly and correctly to an opponent
- the motivation to succeed despite fatigue and injury.

A typical competition requires non-repetitive work over a period of 2 or 3 minutes, except in taekwondo, and full contact where there is a series of rounds. Competition consists of periods of low activity interspersed with sudden and violent onslaughts. During these active phases, controlled techniques are delivered with maximum speed and agility.

To do well in a competition from the fitness point of view, the student requires:

- to be mentally and physically prepared for the competition
- the ability to work very hard in intervals for perhaps 1 or 2 minutes
- the ability to use techniques quickly and accurately
- the ability to respond very quickly to the opponent
- the flexibility to use the required techniques
- the motivation not to be a good loser.

The coach must decide in what proportions these various fitness components are mixed.

Assessing fitness

This is unlikely to figure largely in the average martial art coach's programme at the present time, since he ordinarily deals with large classes where training proceeds at an overall pace. In all-novice classes, for example, the pace is slower than in advanced classes and is geared to the abilities of the majority, so the good coach will constantly monitor performance and will adjust pace where necessary. A knowledge of fitness assessment may, however, become important when the coach is involved in the rehabilitation of a top performer after injury, or in the close-up training of a private student.

By running a fitness programme concurrently with training it follows that intermediate and advanced classes have higher levels both of skill and of fitness. Increase in skill will be measured at the grading examination, whilst increase in fitness shows itself through acceleration in training pace. The fitter student can perform more techniques with more power, agility and co-ordination than his less fit colleague in the course of a lesson.

As a practical assessment of the fitness component, the coach can monitor the class to see what percentage is flagging. If the work-rate of the advanced class is not significantly greater than that of the intermediates, then fitness is not improving at the same rate as skill.

Though useful for the experienced coach, this type of assessment is similar to a grading examination in that it is subjective. This is to say that one coach might consider that the class is working hard whilst another might think the students are slacking. Where there is a need to make an objective assessment of fitness (that is, one which is actually measurable in physical terms), a number of different methods can be used. Before starting on these, ask yourself the following questions:

a   what aspect of fitness do you want to assess?

b   how will you measure that aspect?
c   why do you think an assessment will be useful?
d   what will you do once you have analysed the results?

Let's select an imaginary taekwondo class as the subject of a fitness assessment. You as coach might very well want to assess hip flexibility in connection with the height of kicks. You might decide to measure it by seating the subject on the floor with legs spread as wide as possible and then reading off the distance between heels with a tape measure (*see photograph 3*). This will serve as the baseline on which to check the success of a flexibility programme. The same students should be tested half-way through and at the end of the programme. Since you have their starting measurements, you can show how training has improved hip flexibility.

Not only does this provide positive vindication of the training method you are using, an improvement also increases motivation amongst the tested students. They can see for themselves that as a result of your training they *are* improving. Begin by comparing increased performance in the assessment on an individual basis. Don't compare two different students because response to the programme may vary greatly between individuals.

Having said that, if you perform the same assessments for year after year with different classes, you may begin to detect a trend. For example, over a period of 2 years, you may split each beginners' class in half on a random basis and give a 3-month flexibility programme to one half (the 'Test Group') and no programme to the other (the 'Control Group'). Measure both groups at the start, half-way through the 3 months and at the end of the programme. Record the results from both groups.

At the end of the 2 years, you will have a respectable volume of data from which to draw some conclusions. For example, you can say that the flexibility programme resulted in a good increase in flexibility, but that when you compared it with the control group, the increase was less obvious.

3. Measuring hip flexibility by checking the distance between heels

To get the best results from this type of valuable analysis, watch out for errors which can arise if you:

- don't identify a target age/sex group to test. If you decide to test everybody in the beginners' class, then one class may contain a higher than usual proportion of school children – all of whom will tend to have greater hip flexibility than a corresponding group of adults. Assess the class on the basis of discrete sex and age groups
- don't select the test and control groups randomly from within each of the categories you have laid down. Any attempt to influence the selection will bias the results obtained from that assessment
- don't conduct the assessment at the same time of day and point in training. If you make one assessment for flexibility before warm-up and a second one afterwards, you will see a difference in the same student in the same evening!
- don't run the assessment programme over a long enough time and/or with a large enough number of students. Smaller clubs may have to run assessments for longer periods to get enough results.

The Martial Arts Commission looks forward to receiving a flood of reports on objective assessments of martial art training methods. From this will come the core of technical knowledge which is so lacking in the martial arts.

The warm-up and cool-down

Consider the student who works in an office all day. Her body will be geared to work at that pace, yet once she begins training her muscles will have to work harder, her joints bend more fully and frequently and both heart rate and respiration will accelerate.

Certainly, she can come straight in, get changed and launch immediately into training, though if she does she may experience discomfort as her body acclimatises. The unprepared muscles may be sluggish at first and the joints stiff through lack of use. Heavy exertion during the first few moments of training from cold may actually cause injuries, so for these reasons it is better to raise the body's preparedness gradually by means of a programme of exercises known as the 'warm-up'. Actually, this is a misnomer, because with the exception of a slight rise in the temperature of working muscle, nothing actually 'warms up', though you may get red in the face and feel rather sweaty. The body's core temperature is maintained accurately regardless of activity, so an alternative and more appropriate expression might be 'loosening (or limbering) up'. Using actual techniques in the final phases of a vigorous warm-up may help improve skill.

A suggested general warm-up is included on pages 46–67 and you will see that it consists, firstly, of whole body exercises that raise the heart and respiration rate. These are followed by more specific exercises aimed at getting the muscles of the upper body, abdomen and legs to contract more powerfully. Finally, the muscles will be stretched in a general programme that works the whole body.

The intensity and duration of the warm-up will vary according to the average standard of the class and length of the lesson, but the objective is to get the students sweaty and raring to go. Avoid too heavy a warm-up schedule that causes fatigue and ruins the ensuing training. This is particularly important when training beginners' classes containing very unfit people. The best way to assess the exercise loading is to have the class measure their pulse rates (see later in the book) and to compare it with the table. Avoid also the reverse situation, i.e. a warm-up that is too short, because then its benefits will not be fully realised.

The warm-up should take into account the training planned for the lesson. For example, if there is to be a lot of high kicks practised, then it is pointless spending a great deal of time in the warm-up concentrating on the upper body.

The mind benefits from a warm-up, too, in that the student comes to the training hall with everyday attitudes, behaviour patterns and concerns. Before the lesson proper begins, these must be blanked out, because what is acceptable in the street may not be suitable for the training hall. Therefore, the warm-up will include a focusing of attention.

Use an exercise session to break periods of skill training. Specific flexibility exercises are well tolerated after the muscles have been working over a period.

Picture now, if you will, our office worker at the end of a hard training session. Her heart is pounding along and her muscles are fatigued through exertion. Her body will take time to return to its normal level of operation and the products of fatigue must be moved out of the muscles. This can be facilitated by means of a short programme of exercises known as the 'cool-down' (or 'tapering off').

Gradually ease down on the level of activity as your lesson comes to an end, reducing the power of techniques until they become almost like exercises. A schedule of general cool-down exercises is given on page 67. It includes a programme of gently stretching the muscles you have been using during the lesson. The tempo must gradually slow as the programme comes to its end. Follow a hard training session with a long soak in a hot bath.

The cool-down must also work on the mind, training students to keep martial art techniques in the training hall – not in the street or in the playground.

Training methods to avoid

To conclude this chapter, I want to discuss common training faults which occur in martial art training.

It is an unfortunate fact that in many martial art associations to my personal knowledge, senior teaching personnel have little or no knowledge of physiology and fitness training. Here are some of the faults I have noticed:

■ children are made to do press-ups on their knuckles or backs of their hands

- young people are made to train for woodbreaking
- flexibility training is not accompanied by muscle building exercises
- injurious ballistic flexibility methods are in common usage
- incorrect leg power training which over-stresses the knee joint is common
- incorrect strength training exercises which injure the lower back and stomach occur frequently.

Let's now consider these in detail.

Firstly, children are not miniature adults. They do not have the same levels and types of fitness as adults because their physiology differs. They are building new tissues and consequently have less energy available for training. Thus a child may be able to sustain a low level of training well enough, yet be incapable of lasting a prolonged and hard training session. The child's bones are not fully formed and adult exercises can cause permanent damage. This is simply not realised by many martial art instructors.

Under X-ray examination, the child's wrist looks quite different from an adult's (*see photograph 4*). The wrist bones are not fully formed and the joint relies upon cartilage for its form and movement. Press-ups on the back of the hand over-stress and damage this cartilage, which means that when the bones eventually harden, they are deformed and wrist mobility may be affected.

Press-ups on the knuckles can damage the growing points of young finger bones, also resulting in permanent damage. Repeatedly smashing the fist into wood causes the same damage, but more quickly and thoroughly.

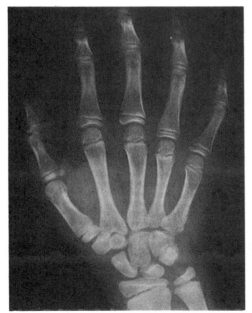 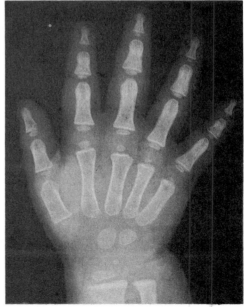

4. *Left* X-ray of an adult's wrist and hand; *right* X-ray of a child's wrist and hand

Young people are generally more flexible than adults. They perform high kicks, for example, with consummate ease. However, flexibility training stretches the muscles holding joints together and if this training is not accompanied by the correct form of muscle strengthening, then those young martial artists are going to grow up with unstable (i.e. 'wobbly') joints. Even in adults, flexibility training *must* be accompanied by appropriate muscle strengthening.

Stretching exercises are widespread in martial art practice. They are commonly associated with bouncing to apply extra pressure to the muscles being stretched. We will consider the mechanism of stretching a little later, but for now suffice it to say that in all but the most highly trained martial artists this bouncing is likely to have, at best, little improvement value and, at worse, a negative effect.

I have seen instructors stand on students' knees during exercises to stretch the muscles along the inside of the thighs. This is potentially very injurious and must not be done. Slightly less horrific but injurious just the same, are instructors jerking students' legs violently out to the side during box-splits.

Exercises to develop powerful upper leg muscles are common to many martial arts. Often these take the form of bunny-hops, or squats with added weight. When the knee joint is bent even a few degrees under body weight, the stress on its components is many times body weight. When the angle of the knee bend passes 90 degrees, that loading is increased to a level where injury becomes a possibility. It is for this reason that bunny-hops should be avoided and squats should be stopped at the half-way point (*see photograph 5*).

The possibility of knee injury is increased both when the body is loaded with

5. The knee joints should not be bent further than 90° during exercise to develop upper leg muscles

additional weight and when the martial artist drops to his haunches and immediately bounces back up again. This adds an unwelcome ballistic component to an already over-stressed knee joint.

Lack of knowledge of physiology sometimes means that a martial art instructor is confused over the effect of an exercise, believing it does one thing when, in fact, it does another. Take, for example, the basic sit-up. This is most often practised for its abdominal training effect. Students lie on their backs, with legs extended and perhaps held down by a partner (*see photograph 6*). They lurch up off the ground and fold forwards as far as they can manage before dropping back. Let's now analyse this.

To throw the shoulders clear of the ground, the back arches and the pelvis tilts forwards, allowing the powerful long muscles on the front of the thighs to add their strength to the abdominal muscles. Once the trunk reaches a vertical position, its further movement forwards does not strengthen the abdominals.

Firstly, the tilting of the pelvis prior to launch is injurious to the lower back. Secondly, if the exercise is intended to work the abdominal muscles, then it is only partially successful because the thigh muscles are involved when they shouldn't be. Contrast this with a sit-up from bent knees where the objective is merely to lift the shoulders and upper back clear of the ground (*see photograph 7*). This version works the abdominal muscles more intensively and so achieves more effectively what the instructor has in mind.

Before leaving this topic, let me tell you about one amazing abdominal exercise I have come across. This consists of putting the class side by side on their backs and having the end ones run over the stomachs of the rest! The effects of a heavy person jumping onto a child I leave to your fertile imagination. I have also seen the runner momentarily lose balance and step squarely into the groin of one unlucky soul. Ouch!

Questions

1 What is fitness?
2 What does 'physiology' mean?
3 List the benefits that correct fitness training brings to martial art practice.
4 List the factors that comprise fitness and briefly explain each one.
5 How do age, sex and heredity affect training?
6 List the ways that training can affect fitness.
7 During a 90-minute training session, how much time would you devote to fitness training?
8 Describe the fitness requirements of training, grading and competition (if applicable) in your martial art.
9 Is there any relationship between the exercises selected and the techniques/training they are supposed to improve?
10 Give an example of how a fitness assessment could benefit your students.
11 What is a 'Control Group'?

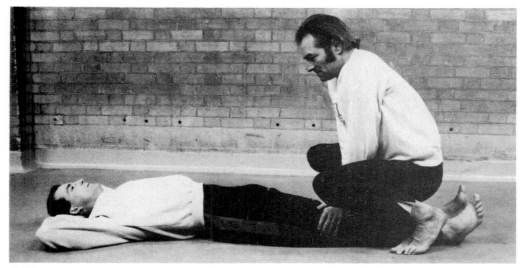

6. The wrong way to begin sit-ups

7. The right way to do sit-ups

12   What are the pitfalls to avoid when interpreting fitness assessments?
13   What is the purpose of the warm-up?
14   Describe a typical warm-up programme and mention the faults to avoid.
15   What is the purpose of the cool-down?
16   List some common fitness training faults.
17   What exercises are unsuitable for young people, and why?
18   What form of training must accompany flexibility work?

PRACTICAL WARM-UP
AND COOL-DOWN PROGRAMMES

The warm-up

The following schedule of exercises will ensure that students are properly prepared for the demands of training. Match the exercises, number of repetitions and duration of practice to the time available, to the class's overall fitness and to the format of the ensuing lesson. Remember that the purpose of the warm-up is to bring the body safely into a position where it can act powerfully throughout its normal range of movement. Contrast this with body preparation which sets out to **extend** the body's limits.

1 Begin the warm-up by making the class run on the spot, raising their knees high and allowing their arms to move naturally. This will work muscles and joints.
2 Make the class stand with feet a shoulder-width apart and turned slightly outwards. On the command, they must drop into a half-squat (*see photograph 8*), pausing there before driving quickly up again. Don't allow them to drop

8. Drop into a half-squat

9. On the tenth jump, knees are pulled into the chest

below a half-squat, because this strains the knee joint unnecessarily. Make them pause at the lowest point, because this increases the training effect and reduces knee loadings produced through a ballistic effect.

3 Then make the students jump up and down off the balls of their feet, at the same time keeping their arms by their sides. Every tenth jump must be made as high as possible, pulling the knees to the chest (*see photograph 9*). By this time the class will be quite warm.

4 It is now possible to introduce slightly more arduous exercises. Make the class perform **star jumps**, extending their arms and legs as widely as possible (*see photograph 10*). A full recovery is made before landing.

5 Maintain the accelerating pace of exercises by introducing **burpees**. Students begin from an upright position, and drop into a crouch, with the tips of their fingers brushing the ground (*see photograph 11*). The legs are driven out behind and the body is supported on straight arms (*see photograph 12*). The legs are brought back before driving upright once more.

6 Divide the class into teams, with students sprinting to the far wall and coming to a stop before returning to the rear of the line to start the next student running.

7 Keeping the relay teams, set the students skipping from side to side with

10. Extend arms and legs to perform a star jump

11. Starting position for a burpee

12. From the starting position, drive the legs out whilst supporting the body on straight arms

alternating single leg leaps (*see photograph 13*) until they reach the far wall, returning to start the next in line. Alternatively, make them swing the advancing leg across the front of the other (*see photograph 14*).

8　Work the upper body with **press-ups**, allowing beginners to drop their knees to the ground if necessary (*see photograph 15*). Check that students are supporting themselves on the tips of their toes and on the flats of their hands, keeping their bodies in one straight line. Check for sagging in the middle or hips lifted well clear of the ground. On the command, drop until the chest brushes the

Above 13. Side skipping

Right 14. Front leg swinging across the back leg

15. If necessary, beginners can drop their knees to the ground during press-ups

16. Drop the chest until it brushes the floor during the press-up

floor (*photograph 16*). Pause at that point to maximise training effect. Then forcefully drive back up to lock the arms once more. Don't allow bouncing down, because this both reduces training effect and loads the elbows unnecessarily. Watch out for cheating as the class grows tired.

9   More advanced students can drop to the low position and, after the pause, drive powerfully up so that their hands come clear of the floor. Students with powerful upper body musculature should be encouraged to clap their hands together as they come free.

10   Further vary the training effect of press-ups by making the class spread their hands wider than shoulder-width (*photograph 17*), or taking them forwards from the shoulders (*photograph 18*). Conversely, make them bring their hands into the lower mid-section (*photograph 19*). One-handed press-ups can also be practised by the most advanced class (*photograph 20*).

11   Keep everyone in the press-up position, but ask them to arch their backs

17. Vary the effect of the press-up by spreading the hands further than shoulder-width . . .

18. ... or by taking them forwards

Right 19. ... or by bringing them into the centre

Below 20. ... or one-handed press-ups can be performed

21. Arching the back in the press-up position

22. Bending the elbows

(*photograph 21*). On command, they bend their elbows so the body skims forwards just above the ground (*photograph 22*). Then the elbows are straightened and the hips are dropped (*photograph 23*), after which the starting posture is resumed by reversing the sequence of movements. These movements are called **cat stretches**.

23. Straightening the elbows and dropping the hips

12 Divide the class in half for sit-ups, putting one half on their backs with knees bent and the other half holding their ankles down (*photograph 24*). Make the working partners clasp their hands behind their heads, but ensure they don't

24. Sit-ups, making use of a partner

tug hard as they come up. Impress on them that all the work should be done by the abdominal muscles, so there is no need to continue up until foreheads touch knees. Encourage the class not to jerk into the exercise and have them pause at the position of maximum loading before dropping back. Don't allow them to flop back and then immediately to spring up again.

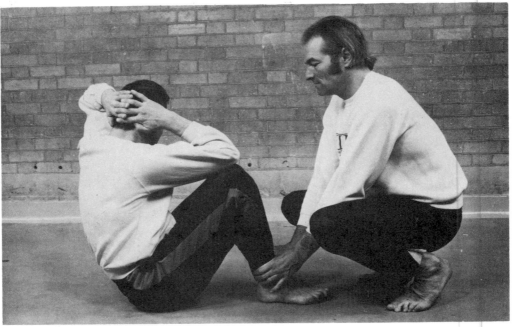

25. Varying the effect of a sit-up by twisting the trunk

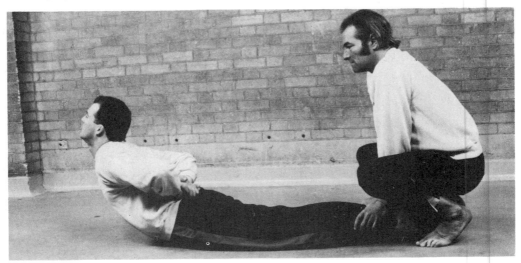

26. The back hyper-extension exercise

13 Keeping the class in pairs, vary the training effect of sit-ups by asking the students to rotate their trunks *(photograph 25)*, touching the right knee with the left elbow. On the next rise, they touch the left knee with the right elbow.

14 Keep the class in pairs. Active partners roll onto their front, grasping their hands either in the small of the back or behind the head. The inactive partners press down on the heels to prevent the feet from rising. On your command, the class raise their chests clear of the ground by arching their backs *(photograph 26)*. Warn them against raising too far, because the straining this involves often causes dizziness. The exercise is named the **back hyper-extension**.

15 Next, the class performs **side stretches** from a feet-apart position. On command, the students lean first to one side *(photograph 27)*, and then to the other. The arms are used to add body weight to the upper body. Don't allow the students to jerk into the stretch, but aim for a smooth progression into the lowest position, holding this for a few seconds before returning to an upright position.

16 Keep the class in the same stance, but this time ask them to twist their bodies first to one side *(photograph 28)*, and then to the other. Check that the movement is slow and also that maximum stretch is maintained for a couple of seconds.

27. Side stretching

28. Twisting to the right

29. Holding maximum stretch

30. Reaching between splayed legs

31. Going into a back hyper-extension

32. Trunk circling

17 Vary the stretch by making the class bend forwards, using the weight of their hanging arms to drag down (*photograph 29*). Note that some students have long arms and short legs, as well as vice versa! Students must hold maximum stretch before returning to the upright stance.

18 Further vary the training effect of the last exercise by asking the students to reach through between their splayed legs (*photograph 30*), holding maximum stretch before straightening into a hyper-extension (*photograph 31*).

19 Begin the next exercise by making the class swing their upper bodies in a wide circle that goes from one side, through into a hyper-extension and finally down the other side (*photograph 32*). Make the students repeat the circle in the opposite direction.

20 Make students lower their body weight over one knee whilst keeping the other knee straight (*photograph 33*). Do not allow them to bounce on the stretched muscle, but ask them to hold it instead at maximum stretch before they repeat the exercise on the other leg.

21 Vary the last exercise by asking students to sink onto their supporting legs (*photograph 34*). They maintain balance by leaning forwards and carrying the hands out as counter-weights. Check that the supporting foot is flat on the floor.

22 Make the class sit down, with their legs together and straight. Ask them to keep the backs of their legs pressed firmly to the ground and then lean forwards as

33. Body weight is lowered over the right knee, whilst the left knee is kept straight

far as possible. They can pull down by grasping their shins (*photograph 35*), or by extending their arms, allowing upper body weight to add to the stretch. The upper body must lean forwards – nodding the head will not suffice. Ask students to hold maximum stretch for at least 10 seconds.

23 Vary the training effect with open-leg stretches. Make students lean between

34. Extend the stretch by sinking down on the supporting leg and leaning forwards. Use the arms as counter–weights.

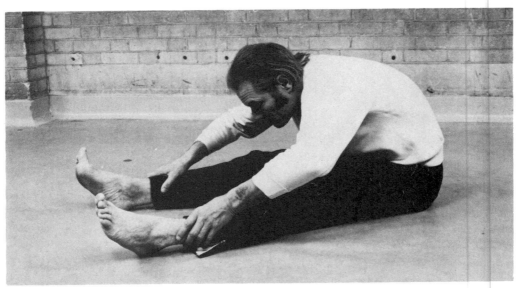

35. To help lean forwards, shins can be grasped

their outstretched legs and assist the stretch by pushing their extended arms forwards (*photograph 36*). Ask them to hold maximum stretch for at least 10 seconds. Watch for bent knees and the upper body not leaning forwards. Vary the exercise by first leaning towards one knee (*photograph 37*), and then to the other.

36. Reach well forward during the open-leg stretch

37. Leaning towards the right knee during an open-leg stretch

38. Reaching forwards over the left knee

39. Bending towards the right knee

40. Bending forwards between the knees

24 Ask the class to sit, each with left leg extended and right knee bent and to the side. Either by leaning forwards and using bodyweight, or with a partner assisting, students must reach forwards past their left foot. Make them curl their fingers around the heel to hold maximum stretch (*photograph 38*). They must return to an upright position and then bend towards their right knee (*photograph 39*) which is grasped with both hands. Ask them to hold maximum position as before. Finally, they must dip their head between their knees, resting it against the floor (*see photograph 40*).

25 Make the class gather their feet close to their thighs whilst grasping their ankles. On command, they must lean between their knees whilst pulling smoothly down with their hands (*photograph 41*). Ask them to hold maximum stretch before straightening.

26 Keep the class in a sitting position, and ask them to take one leg across the other and grasp the ankle (*photograph 42*). This is then rotated in a wide circle, going first one way, and then the other.

41. Pulling with the hands whilst leaning between the knees

42. Rotating the ankle

27 Make the students roll backwards onto their shoulders and extend their legs. They brace this position with splayed arms on either side (*photograph 43*). Vary the exercise by asking the students to open their legs wide (*photograph 44*).

28 Further vary the training effect of the last exercise by asking students to drop their legs first to one side (*photograph 45*), and then to the other.

29 Ask the class to adopt a kneeling position, with feet extended and back straight (*photograph 46*). This stretches the long muscles on the front of the thighs and also improves ankle extension. Make the class hold this position for at least 30 seconds.

30 Keep the class in a kneeling position and ask them to increase stretch by leaning back until their shoulders rest on the ground (*photograph 47*). Their knees must be kept pressed to the floor.

43. Roll back onto the shoulders and extend the legs

44. Open the legs wide, but keep the knees fully extended

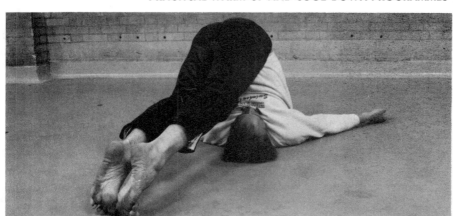

45. Vary the exercise by dropping the feet either side of the head

46. Kneeling, with straight back and extended feet

47. Leaning back to rest the shoulders on the floor

31 Ask the class to stand up and place their hands on bent knees. They must rotate their legs in wide circles, going first one way, and then the other (*photograph 48*).

32 Make the students place their hands on their hips and rotate their lower trunks in wide circles, first one way (*photograph 49*), and then the other.

33 Next, ask the students to move their arms in slow and full contra-rotating circles (*photograph 50*).

48. Rotating the hips in wide circles, keeping the hands on bent knees

Below left 49. Rotating the hips first one way, then the other: hands can be placed on the hips

Below 50. Contra-rotating shoulder swings

34 Ask the students to work their wrists so that the little finger is brought towards the chest (*photograph 51*). Next, make them point their fingers away from the body whilst trying to rotate the hand palm-upwards (*photograph 52*). Vary the stretch yet further by asking the class to turn their fingers downwards and pull back on the palms (*photograph 53*).

51. Twisting the wrist

Below left 52. Working the lateral movement of the wrist

Below right 53. Over-extending the wrist

35 Conclude the warm-up with neck exercises, asking students to drop their heads to one side, and then to the other (*photograph 54*). Next, make them perform a twisting exercise that turns the head one way, and then the other (*photograph 55*). Finish off by making students nod their heads forwards, and then backwards (*photograph 56*).

54. Laterally flex the neck joint

Below left 55. Twisting the neck joint

Below 56. Roll the head first one way, then the other

This list of exercises is far from complete, but it will serve as a menu from which coaches can select those relevant to training.

Martial art training itself can be used very effectively to warm up the class. In this case, normal techniques are performed quickly but without power. For example, students practise roundhouse kicks against a target mitt held at head height. The kicks are rapid and follow each other quickly, yet there is no power in the impacts. Similarly, flurries of fast relaxed punches quickly loosen the upper body, warning the tissues of what they will shortly be subjected to in the lesson proper. This form of warm-up can actually increase skill.

The cool-down

The cool-down gradually returns working muscles from their active condition to a normal one. The fluids and waste products which have built up during training can be pumped out by continuing with training techniques which have been deliberately de-tuned. Alternatively, perform exercises such as 1, 2, 3, 8, 12 and 14. Select also stretching exercises, such as 15, 16, 17, 19, 20, 21, 22, 23, 24, 25, 28, 33 and 34.

Perform these with a slowing tempo and without the need for great exertion. Advise the class to replenish fluid lost during training.

THE PHYSIOLOGY OF FITNESS TRAINING

The first priority of fitness training

How many of us have permanent joint injury as a result of poor training? I have two knees which occasionally give trouble. Other senior martial artists of my acquaintance suffer from back, knee and/or elbow conditions. Many others, I am sure, would not come out well if their joint function now was compared with what it was before they began training – allowing, of course, for normal deterioration through age.

Whilst a couple of ropey joints after 25 years of training hardly commends martial art practice as a healthy pastime, what about the 12-year-old black belt lad who has just had his knee cartilages removed? He is only one of many young people injured through bad coaching. Such cases as this are needless. They can be effectively combatted by a knowledge of basic physiology, correct skill training and body conditioning exercises.

Whereas many fitness training regimes take as their priority the need to increase power, flexibility and endurance in relation to skill requirements, I believe our first and most important priority by far is to help the body withstand the rigours of training. As I have indicated, the body's joints are particularly vulnerable to stresses imposed by training and I am therefore concentrating first on this aspect of fitness.

Muscles and ligaments ensure that the bearing surfaces of joints correctly locate against each other, so maintaining a full range of movement and reducing undue wear and tear.

Ligaments respond slightly to training and, though elastic, they can nevertheless be over-stretched. When this happens, they don't return to their previous length and the joint may not locate so securely thereafter. This is most obviously seen in ankle injuries where following a bad sprain, subsequent sprains happen with less provocation. As a means of reducing ligamentous damage, there is simply no substitute for martial art skill plus a knowledge of physiology.

The muscles associated with joint function can be strengthened, and a programme which sets out to do just that is definitely worthwhile.

The best muscle strengthening exercises for joints are isometrically based. These use muscular contraction without joint movement – as, for example, when you try to push a car that has been left in gear and with the handbrake on. Used properly, isometrics are very good at improving muscular tone, though you must vary the joint angle through which the muscles are acting to get the best result. Muscle tone is the level of contraction maintained in apparently inactive muscle, and it is a major contributor to muscle strength.

The flexibility part of the training refers to the relaxation and stretching of these same muscles – so you see immediately that both programmes must always go hand in hand. Moreover, do please realise that more than one muscle is associated with each joint: therefore, training must work all of them equally.

Choose exercises which do not over-stress the joint by looking at how that joint functions, and then working it in that function. Let's begin by considering the way the joints of the body work.

The spine

The spinal column rises up from the pelvis to the head. It is made up of 33 bones known as **vertebrae** and, for convenience sake, these are further divided from the bottom up into **coccygeal** (4 vertebrae), **sacral** (5 vertebrae), **lumbar** (5 vertebrae), **thoracic** (12 vertebrae) and **cervical** (7 vertebrae). The coccygeal vertebrae are fused together into a short and rudimentary tail which is incapable of movement and therefore does not concern us.

The sacral vertebrae are also fused together, but they do concern us insofar as the joint they make with the pelvis – the **sacro–iliac** – is capable of a limited front-to-back rocking movement. The muscles associated with the sacro–iliac will benefit from strengthening exercises and I have listed one on page 91. Don't leave them out of your programme, because training does place severe strains on this joint and injury to it is both long-term and troublesome.

The remaining spinal vertebrae are free to move against each other to a greater or lesser degree, by this means providing an overall flexibility. They are, however, held firmly together both by muscles, which attach to each vertebra's bony spines, and by ligaments. Between each vertebra is a plate of reinforced cartilage containing a jelly-filled damping system which reduces the jarring associated with movement. This plate is the 'spinal disc' – which has been known to 'slip' occasionally. Interestingly, vertebrae can be surgically fused together without major loss of spinal movement. One senior martial artist of my acquaintance required surgery to his spine, in which vertebrae were fixed together with steel rods. Despite this, he trains vigorously and without apparent difficulty.

The thoracic vertebrae of the chest support the ribs and cervical vertebrae give the head a wide range of movement. Let's now look at the directions in which the spine can move.

First of all you can bend forwards to touch your toes in the action known as 'flexion'. This mainly involves the cervical and lumbar regions. Straighten up and push your hips forward so that you are looking into the sky. This is 'extension' (*photograph 57*) and it, too, is mainly produced in the cervical and lumbar regions.

57. This is spinal extension . . .

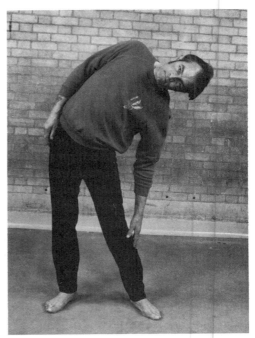

58. . . . and this is lateral flexion

59. Spinal rotation happens when you twist around

60. Spinal rotation takes the back through a full range of movement

You can lean to the side and this is a movement called 'lateral flexion' (*photograph 58*) which involves most of the spine to a greater or lesser degree. You can twist to look behind you in the action named 'rotation' (*photograph 59*), using mainly the cervical and upper thoracic vertebrae. Trunk rotation in big circles (*photograph 60*) is named 'circumduction'.

Examine these separate movements and consider how exercises which both strengthen and improve suppleness in the spine can be used. Compare your analysis with the schedule given on pages 91–5.

The shoulder

The shoulder is a ball and socket joint with a large range of movement. It is stabilised by strong muscles and will benefit from proper training, being most at risk in those martial arts which use throwing and joint-locking techniques.

'Flexion' of the shoulder occurs when you raise your arm from a hanging position at your side and lift it to the front. It is returned the same way to your side in the action named 'extension' (*photograph 61*). The shoulder is also capable of horizontal flexion and extension (*photograph 62*) by holding the arm out horizontally whilst moving it across your chest and pulling it back.

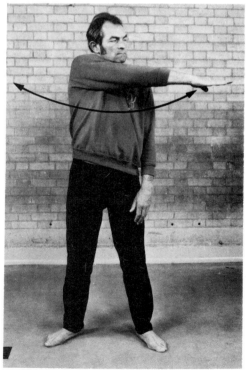

61. Raising the arm is shoulder flexion; lowering it is shoulder extension

62. Horizontal flexion and extension of the right shoulder

Now lift your arm out and away from your side. This is 'abduction'. Returning it (*photograph 63*) is 'adduction'. Roll your arm around in a wide circle to perform 'circumduction' (*photograph 64*). Bend your elbow to a right angle and swing the forearm horizontally inwards (internal rotation) and outwards (external rotation – *see photograph 65*).

63. Abduction and adduction of the right shoulder

Below left 64. Circumduction of the right shoulder
Below 65. External rotation of the shoulders

The elbow

This joint frequently gives trouble during training, especially in those martial arts which punch hard against no resistance. If this is wrongly done, the bones of the elbow limit arm extension and eventual damage is likely. No joint conditioning programme can prevent this damage; rather a change to a more sensible training method is required.

The elbow is essentially a hinge joint, stabilised both by its bony structure and by elastic ligaments. These allow it to move in four directions, the first two being flexion and extension (*see photograph 66*). It is during extension that injury is most likely to occur.

The bones of the lower arm can rotate over each other in the region of the elbow, allowing you to turn your palm upwards ('supination') and downwards ('pronation' – *see photograph 67*). During a punching action, the elbow both extends and pronates.

Some martial artists consider that the wrist is responsible for rotating the fist from palm-up to palm-down positions, but this, of course, is incorrect.

66. Flexion and extension of the right elbow

67. Pronation of the right elbow: the palm turns downwards

The wrist

The wrist suffers most in those martial arts specialising in joint-locking techniques and neither novice nor high grade is immune to injury. Whilst wrist exercises are especially important to these arts, they should not be omitted from the striking-based counterparts.

The wrist can flex and extend (*see photograph 68*). It can even abduct and adduct slightly from side to side, an action used during hooking blocks.

68. Flexion and extension of the right wrist

69. Extension of the fingers into spear hand

The fingers

The fingers are used in every martial art, though it is in the grappling-based forms where they are perhaps most used. The fingers and thumb are easily damaged, especially when blocking and there is no substitute for good technique.

The fingers can flex and extend (*see photograph 69*) and, in addition, each is capable of limited side-to-side movement. The thumb has a greater range of movement, crossing the palm of the hand in an action named 'opposition'.

The hip

Like the shoulder, the hip is a ball and socket joint with a wide range of movement. The healthy person's hip joint is deeply seated and is held firmly by muscles and ligaments. The requirements of normal activity work the joint effectively, but additional flexibility work is nearly always needed to facilitate martial art practice. When you lift your knee prior to a front kick (*see photograph 70*), you are performing hip flexion. As you retrieve the kick and return it to the start position, you are extending the joint. Abduction of the hip occurs when your knee lifts to the side during side-kick (*photograph 71*), and dropping it back the same way constitutes adduction. Those of us who perform those spectacular circular kicks (*photograph 72*) are demonstrating circumduction.

You can also turn your foot from side to side through internal and external rotation (*photograph 73*).

70. Hip flexion, by lifting the right knee before kicking forwards

71. Abduction of the right hip

72. Circumduction of the right hip

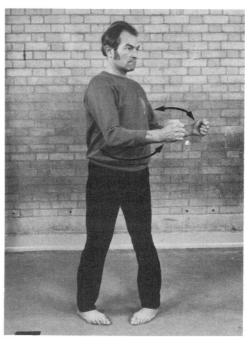

73. Internal rotation of the hips

74. Straddle stance in which the knees are turned inwards

75. Knee joints can be damaged when made to bend further than 90° during exercises

76. Front kick, showing extension of the right knee

The knee

The knee is perhaps the most vulnerable joint in the body to injury, whether or not an individual is practising a martial art. It is essentially a hinge joint stabilised by powerful muscles but controlled by the ligaments. The latter are easily stretched, causing abnormal joint movement with attendant damage to the cartilage.

It is easily damaged during unrestrained kicks, when the lower leg slams out straight. It also takes none too kindly to stances which put a lateral strain on it, such as that variety of low straddle stance where the feet are rotated inwards (*photograph 74*). Strain across the joint multiplies according to its angle and damage is most likely when it is regularly bent more than 90 degrees, and then made to work against a weight (*photograph 75*).

The knee is capable of only two movements – extension and flexion (*see photograph 76*).

The ankle

The ankle is a composite joint made up of many small bones held together by ligaments and stabilised by muscles. Principal range of movement occurs in the directions of 'plantar-' and 'dorsi-flexion' (*see photograph 77*). There is a small amount of lateral movement known as 'eversion' and 'inversion' (*see photograph 78*), both of which are sometimes used in martial art techniques, such as side kick and foot sweep.

Additionally, the whole foot can be rotated in a form of circumduction.

77. Plantar flexion of the right ankle

78. The ankle is also capable of lateral movement – eversion and inversion

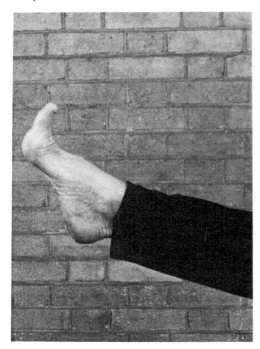

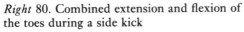
Above 79. Flexing the toes during a front kick

Right 80. Combined extension and flexion of the toes during a side kick

The toes

The toes are often damaged in the impact-based martial arts and can only be safeguarded by good technique. They are hinge joints capable of extension or flexion (*photograph 79*). A combination of both movements is used in the side-kick technique (*photograph 80*). The big toe can also move slightly from side to side, but this has no significance to martial arts practice.

Use the information given above and the exercises suggested on pages 119–40 to create a training programme which can be incorporated into the more general training routines that follow.

The second priority

The second priority of fitness training is to make good any fitness deficit the students may have with respect to the requirements of their martial art activity. Once the desired level of fitness is reached, the coach must know how to maintain it.

Coaches must be capable of determining areas where improvements other than skill are required, and then must know how to set out a programme to make them. Designing such a programme requires an understanding of how the body reacts to various training.

I will now describe some of the components of fitness in more detail and will explain how training affects them.

Aerobic endurance

Aerobic endurance is a product of:

- the lungs' efficiency at exchanging oxygen from the air for carbon dioxide
- the heart's ability to pump sufficient volumes of blood with sufficient force
- an adequate and continuing supply of blood to the working muscles
- efficient movement of oxygen and food from the blood vessels into the muscles, and of waste products from the latter into the blood vessels
- the proper utilisation of those supplies by the muscle fibres themselves.

Consider the heart first. This is a bag of muscle divided into four pump chambers. Like all muscles, it can be exercised so that its efficiency increases. As you might expect, therefore, regular and effective aerobic training results in a larger heart with bigger chambers, capable of pumping more blood per contraction.

To have this beneficial effect, training must make the heart work over a minimum period of time. To determine how much work is needed in the case of a fairly fit martial artist, add 25 to his age and subtract the total from 220. So, for a fit 27-year-old, exercise should be paced to keep the heart beating at around 168 beats a minute over a 20-minutes session. This should be repeated 3 or 4 times a week. Many beginners will not be able to sustain this heart rate for the full session, because their aerobic fitness levels are too low. If you try to work them at that level, anaerobic muscle activity occurs instead and will soon bring on fatigue. Therefore, set them a lower target. As their aerobic fitness improves, they will be able to sustain a higher heart rate over long periods before anaerobic respiration begins to play a major and fatigue-producing part.

Do not attempt to raise the heart rate too high as you push back the anaerobic threshold. Pulse rates above 180 beats a minute are not efficient, because the heart has no time to fill properly. Taper off hard training rather than stop suddenly, otherwise students may feel momentarily unwell and may possibly even collapse. This happens because during hard training muscle action vigorously pumps back blood to the heart and if this suddenly stops, there is a drop in blood supply to the racing heart.

Use the following formula to calculate the maximum safe sustainable heart rate for your students:

maximum safe sustainable rate = (220 − student's age in years)

Show the students how to monitor their pulse by feeling the wrist just below the thumb. When taking someone else's pulse, use your fingers and not your thumb. Count beats for 10 seconds and multiply by 6 to get a heart rate. You can, of course, count over a longer period for greater accuracy, except that the heart rate may be changing as you do so and may give a false measurement.

As aerobic training progresses, the resting pulse rate may gradually drop. The slowest pulse I ever recorded was a slightly arhythmic 30 beats per minute in a young West Indian karate competitor. The tournament doctor sent him to the local hospital where they diagnosed him as being excessively fit!

Each person has about a gallon of blood circulating in the body, though females have slightly less. That part of the blood which carries most of the oxygen is called **haemoglobin** and this is found within the red blood cells. When saturated, blood can hold up to one-fifth of its volume as oxygen. Depleted blood normally contains one-eighth its volume of oxygen, although this can drop to only one thirty-second in well-trained martial artists. In such cases, the muscles are more efficient at extracting oxygen from the blood supply.

Blood cells live for about 120 days, after which they are broken down and replaced. The condition known as **anaemia** occurs when there is a low level of haemoglobin in the blood. It is not uncommon in female martial artists suffering from prolonged menstruation.

Aerobic training leads to an increase in blood volume of 40%–50% above the norm. However, the number of red blood cells does not rise in direct relationship to this increase in volume, so hard training may produce what appears to be (but is not) anaemia. Increase in blood volume may be useful in that it provides a larger reservoir of fluid to be drawn upon during heavy sweating.

During prolonged aerobic training, the martial artist is taking in and venting large volumes of air through the lungs. When training at high altitudes where the level of oxygen is lower, more breaths are needed to take in sufficient oxygen. Breathing too quickly and too deeply will drop carbon dioxide levels in the blood. This affects blood acid/alkali levels, causing compensating changes to occur.

During hard training and especially before an important match or grading, blood supply to the muscles is increased at the expense of the viscera. As much as 90% of blood normally supplied to the organs is diverted to the muscles by what is called the 'vascular shunt'. This can cause the familiar 'butterflies in the stomach'.

Most of the body's blood is carried in veins and only about 20% is actively pumped around by the arteries. This larger reservoir in the veins feeds the pumping system. Very small blood vessels are called **capillaries** and some are so fine that blood cells have to pass through them in single file. Training markedly increases the number of visible capillaries which supply muscles, making additional oxygen and food available.

The lungs respond less obviously to training. There is only a slight increase in volume, though the muscles which assist expiration (breathing out) do become stronger.

Lungs consist of branching tubes which get gradually smaller and smaller until they end in tiny bags called **alveoli**. The alveoli are supplied with blood through capillaries, and it is across their membranes that transference of oxygen and carbon dioxide occurs. The movement is always from a region of higher concentration to one that is lower and since there is more oxygen in the alveolus than in the capillary, oxygen diffuses into the latter. Carbon dioxide diffuses the other way — out of the blood and into the alveolus.

This process is not immediate. It actually takes a finite time for blood to charge up to full capacity with oxygen and at maximum heart rate there is only barely enough time before blood in the alveolus is replaced. Rapid, shallow respiration is inefficient and it is much better to breathe deeply.

Smoking has an adverse effect on aerobic endurance insofar as it reduces the blood's capacity to carry oxygen and irritates the lining of the lungs, so they become narrow and produce mucus. Those martial artists addicted to tobacco are advised not to smoke for 3 to 4 hours before a heavy session or event. Smoking and maximum performance are incompatible.

Aerobically efficient muscles are the last component of the training system. They are capable of handling the volumes of oxygen and food coming to them in the blood supply, whilst efficiently getting rid of carbon dioxide waste. As I said earlier, aerobic training increases the number of visible capillaries, and as a muscle lengthens and contracts it acts as a mechanical blood pump.

As oxygen penetrates into the muscle, it is taken up by **myoglobin**, a substance similar to the haemoglobin in blood. Myoglobin supplies the working muscle cell with oxygen. Aerobic training seems to increase levels of myoglobin by up to 200%. Training at altitude has the same effect.

Not all muscle cells have the same ability to use oxygen. Most efficient users are the so-called 'slow twitch' red fibres. Their colouration comes from associated myoglobin. Not so efficient are 'fast twitch' yellow muscle fibres and least efficient of all in terms of oxygen usage are fast twitch white fibres. The relative numbers of each fibre type in a muscle are fixed as part of our physical make-up.

Aerobic training distinctly affects the internal structure of muscle cells, leading to greater usage of oxygen. Even martial artists with relatively few red fibres will benefit from aerobic training, because of its beneficial effects on fast twitch yellow fibres.

As the muscles work, they gradually use up their energy store of **glycogen** and have to turn to fats. The changeover from one energy source to another may well lead to feelings of fatigue. Moreover, extra oxygen is required to unlock the energy in fats.

Muscle cells also gradually use up supplies of other raw materials, so contraction slows and the relaxation interval between contractions increases. Eventually muscle and joint pain may develop, signalling the need to call a halt.

Refer to pages 116–17 for practical advice on setting up your aerobic programme.

Anaerobic endurance

Unless two people are evenly matched in physique, fitness, skill and aggression, a genuine fight will last only a very short time. There will be a brief flurry of activity using a small number of powerful techniques. The energy source for this comes from within muscles and works without the need for oxygen.

As the muscle fibres' internal energy stores rapidly dwindle, they are pumped back up through what is called 'the phosphagen energy system'. This system quickly runs down and a break of several minutes is required for it to build up again. Correct training will increase the level of energy-pumping phosphagens.

Think of it this way: whereas the aerobic system operates for long periods at lower work-loads, the anaerobic system is geared to maximum effort in a short period. The phosphagen system really does operate over a short period – measurable in seconds only! Of longer duration is a second anaerobic mechanism known as the 'lactic acid system' – sometimes called **glycolysis**.

Glycolysis is less fuel-efficient than the aerobic system, though it remains capable of producing large amounts of energy. Fast twitch white muscle fibres use it and in so doing produce large quantities of the waste product 'lactic acid'. Those martial artists with a high proportion of fast twitch white fibres will tend to produce more lactic acid than those with a low proportion. If this remained in the muscle it would quickly clog up the works, bringing contraction to a stop. A high level in the blood would bring on rapid fatigue after only 3 or 4 minutes' activity.

Though lactic acid is produced in large quantities by martial artists working flat out, it quickly diffuses out of the muscle and into the bloodstream. From there it is filtered off by organs, such as the kidney, and is re-processed back into glucose. Unfortunately, this recycling process cannot keep pace with production and, if there is no rest period, fatigue eventually builds to the point of exhaustion.

To be effective, therefore, the anaerobic training programme must aim to generate large volumes of lactic acid, so the muscles learn to work in the presence of higher levels and the body's feedback regulatory system responds to frequent high doses by increasing the re-processing capability.

All rest periods in anaerobic training must be active. The muscles must be kept pumping, albeit lightly, for it is a fact that muscle blood supply reduces sharply during even short periods of inactivity. When that happens, residual lactic acid is locked in and cause aches and pains.

Practical hints for anaerobic endurance training are given on pages 117–18.

Local muscular endurance

Most of this has already been covered. It is simply the ability of muscles to continue working in spite of fatigue build-up. If you train your leg muscles to deliver lots of kicks, one after the other, then you have improved local muscular endurance in the working muscles. By comparison, the muscles of the chest are little used by this schedule, so they do not fatigue. The reverse happens when you train your arm muscles using repeated punching.

Students practising the Chinese fighting system of **Wing chun kuen** for the first time discover that the muscles of their shoulders, arms and chest quickly become fatigued. The legs are little used by comparison. Therefore, the Wing chun coach will target the involved muscle groups and will work them specifically with endurance exercises so they can cope with training requirements.

Strength

Strength is the force muscles generate against a resistance. There are various forms of strength, just as there are of endurance. The following types can be identified:

a   maximum strength is the greatest force which muscles can exert in a single contraction. In practical terms, this force is not merely a function of the muscle itself but is also related to the mechanical advantage afforded by the leverage it can exert across a joint.

   If you curl a barbell, the maximum strength you can produce will depend upon the angle of the elbow. Assuming that the angle is such as to allow the muscle to contract to its greatest effect, then maximum strength in the contracting muscles is expressed by the heaviest weight that can be curled just once. If too much weight is added, then the biceps bulge but there is no movement of the elbow joint. This, of course, is an isometric contraction.

   Maximum strength will vary from individual to individual. We will never all be capable of exerting the same amount of strength. In fact, relative to other people, we may remain pretty feeble.

b   Strength can be expressed through a slow movement, or through one which expends the same amount of effort in a shorter time interval. This speed of strong contraction is very important in most martial arts. Because the muscle contracts quickly, the load it is capable of moving is less than the maximum. Many martial arts generate strength in the form of a spasm lasting less than a second. In grappling martial arts, this may involve no joint movement, i.e. it is isometric. Isometric spasm of the abdominal muscles is valuable in protecting the viscera from a hard impact technique.

   The spasm is often vocalised through the shout which traditionally accompanies a 'focused' technique. The shout may be soundless – merely a grunt in the back of the throat – or it may be louder. Some martial arts use the shout as a form of war-cry, but that lies outside the scope of our discussion.

c   There is little point in training to deliver one almighty throw, because if it fails, how are you left? Commonsense dictates that you must be able to make repeated techniques with little reduction in the force generated by each. This requires continuous strength, where muscles must work repeatedly at a set level and over a period of time. Compare this with local muscular endurance.

A muscle contracts because it is made up of bundles of minute fibres, each of which is capable of shortening its length in response to a stimulus. As it does so, it grows thicker in girth. When a lot of fibres in a muscle contract together, the overall length of that muscle shortens.

Not all the fibres will shorten under normal training and a reserve of up to 25% is held back. This reserve only comes into operation under extreme emotional stress and motivation. It contributes to the phenomenon known as 'hysterical strength'. Regular usage of this reserve is inadvisable, because it will damage joints, bones, tendons and ligaments. However, effective and progressive strength training both pushes back the reserve threshold and adapts the skeletal system to the additional stresses.

Muscle fibres are separated by an elastic membrane through which pass the capillaries and nerves. These strands of membrane come together towards the end of the muscle and join with tough connective tissue to form a tendon, by which the muscle is attached to a bone. Irrespective of leverage, the theoretical maximum strength that any muscle can generate is related to the number of fibres it contains and the way in which they join the tendons.

Strength training makes the muscles work harder than they customarily do, so they respond by storing extra glycogen, the fibres thicken and the muscle sheath becomes stronger. The ligaments gain in elastic strength and extra calcium phosphate is deposited in bones. Male martial artists undergoing strength training develop swollen muscles through the action of the male hormone **testosterone**. Female martial artists will not respond so obviously.

We anticipate the strength needed to perform a task and then apply it by switching in more and more fibres as load weight is taken up. This nerve/muscle interaction is called a 'feedback mechanism' and it allows us to regulate the application of strength to suit the task.

The muscle thickens as it contracts, and the joint through which it operates moves in response. This is a 'concentric contraction'. Compare it with that which occurs as you carefully lower a weight back down. Your muscles are still straining, even though they are being stretched, and this is an 'eccentric contraction'. It may surprise you to learn that an eccentric contraction is stronger than a concentric contraction of the same muscle.

If a muscle is first eccentrically contracted and then concentrically contracted, its movement is both stronger and faster. This is the principle underlying **plyometrics**. It is an important and as yet largely unexplored avenue of technique development.

Considering how the muscle exerts a varying force according to its stage of contraction, it should be possible to apply a varying load to train maximally the muscle through its full range. This can be achieved on weight training multigyms by means of cams. More expensive machines can vary load so the muscle can contract at a constant and preset speed.

Since both speed and strength contribute to the power of a technique, most martial artists would probably benefit from a general strength programme. Whereas maximum speed for any individual is quickly reached, strength has more scope for improvement.

General strength training is important because it provides a framework on which to do specific work. For example, if you want to strengthen your arms, you will need to work on your legs, too (unless you exercise in a sitting position).

Developing maximum strength requires working with heavy loads over few repetitions. By comparison, developing a fast contraction needs light loads and more repetitions.

I have set out some examples of general strength exercises on pages 119–30.

The first stage in setting up a more specific strength programme is to identify relevant exercises for what you are doing. It is no use strengthening musculature in the wrong way! Therefore, if Jim wants to improve the speed/strength of his roundhouse kick, then rather than use a multigym or bodyweight exercises, he might strap on an ankle weight and do sets of rapid kick repetitions against a target pad. It will not have escaped your notice that at the same time he will be improving both skill acquisition and local muscular endurance.

Consider ways of using:

a   wrist and ankle weights
b   springs and pulleys
c   elastic luggage straps.

Arrange training so that it works on both eccentric and concentric contraction principles.

Make sure that the exercise you devise does not involve a radical departure from the way that technique is normally used. For example, you might decide to strengthen your reverse punch by punching whilst holding a dumb-bell. However, the moving weight may cause you to compensate in a way incompatible with good technique.

Speed

A muscle fibre contracts when microscopic protein fibrils within it slide over each other. This sliding process is driven by the action of molecular 'ratchets' that row the fibrils past each other in what is called **inter-digitation**. The rate at which this rowing action occurs determines the ultimate speed of contraction of that muscle fibre.

There are other factors, of course. The protein myofibrils are surrounded by protoplasm which offers some resistance. As the muscle operates, so it develops heat and active muscles may be up to 3 degrees above average body temperature. Though this doesn't sound much, it does have an effect upon protoplasmic viscosity: it thins it out – just as oil thins out in a hot engine. Warm muscles can contract more quickly and this is yet another reason for a proper warm-up.

Rate of contraction falls as the muscle fatigues, so speed training must involve rested muscles. It must not bring on fatigue and should be individually calibrated so students can perform the exercises at full speed over a set number of repetitions. Two or three sets per training session are sufficient with a full rest between each. The coach must carefully examine the movements to be trained and must devise a relevant drill. For example, competition karate may call for competitors to spring forwards and deliver a fast punch. The spring can be speed-trained using a harness which attaches to the karateka's chest. It has reins which the coach grasps, so he can resist the forward movement.

Punches and kicks should be aimed with an acceptable level of force at a target pad. A punching bag is not particularly suitable for controlled contact martial arts because it tends to produce higher impacts.

Ancient Chinese martial artists trained for faster punches by bending young bamboos and attaching them to their wrists. They would draw back the fist against the pull of the bamboo and then suddenly release it. Tension in the bamboo added to muscle contraction and accelerated the punch into its target. Provided the elbow is not over-extended, the principles used are as valid now as they were then.

Training in water is another way of increasing technique speed, though I don't recommend it for practising groundwork! The national coach of an MAC federal member told me that in parts of Malaysia certain martial art schools make the students wear weighted clothes for long periods of time. He reported that when the weights are removed, students are able to deliver extremely fast techniques.

Owing to a lack of development within the martial arts, there are very few effective and technique-specific speed training drills. Hopefully, this will change in the coming years.

Work also needs to be done on development of speed through analysis of technique. Even the martial artist with few fast twitch fibres can increase speed of his technique through development.

Reaction speed

Reaction speed training uses scenarios which readily transfer to the situation to which you want to react. It is no use practising to press a button in response to a buzzer, for example. It is far better to assume a fighting stance and to react with an effective technique when the buzzer sounds.

As I mentioned in Chapter 2, skill plays a large part in developing a fast reaction time. If you are unfamiliar with the components of a technique, then you must consciously assemble and monitor them during execution, and this radically slows the action. Therefore, the first stage is to attain a high skill level in the techniques to be used. The transference from mental selection to physical action must not be slowed through such things as conflict between training method and effective technique.

The second stage is to recognise and react to the opponent's actions.

When facing an unfamiliar opponent, try to gather as much information as possible about his style. This will help you to recognise cues.

As an example, I trained under an instructor who frequently used a particular sequence of techniques. He would deliver a high roundhouse kick and, if it missed, he'd follow with a back kick to the groin. I became able to recognise the sequence, and one day I waited for the head kick. When it finally came, I swayed back so it missed. Sure enough, in came the back kick – only to find me waiting!

I had discerned a pattern in my instructor's behaviour and was able to react apparently very quickly to the opening cue. Of course, it wasn't actually that I'd reacted faster, it was just that the time lag between seeing a technique, selecting a response and enacting that response had been telescoped right down.

The third factor to consider is the time it takes you to select an appropriate technique from all those milling about in your head. I feel very sorry for those students of martial arts with large syllabuses. The options are many and the selection is therefore longer. Far more immediately effective are those schools with a smaller number of techniques.

One school I know teaches a small number of sophisticated, yet simple, techniques through a practical repetition process which is highly effective in producing very fast automatic reflexes. If the threshold of stimulation is high enough (i.e. an immediate threat is perceived), students launch into a blurred sequence of techniques at a speed which I'm sure they couldn't manage were they to think about it. A way of cheating on reaction time is to select a defence which will work for a wide variety of attacks. This simply guides an unfamiliar attack into a familiar response. Techniques slip through even the most experienced guard. One reason for this is that they fail to trigger a response. Maybe they are travelling apparently too slowly. Perhaps they are approaching from a blind side. Maybe an earlier technique has distracted attention away. All these factors will affect the response.

Flexibility

Flexibility is the range of movement at a joint. The average child is more flexible than the average adult. Boys and girls begin to lose their flexibility after 12 years of age, though girls tend to retain better trunk and hip flexibility than boys. Excessive flexibility training with very young students can damage developing bones and can produce actual deformity. It can also lead to hypermobile, or 'wobbly' joints.

As we have seen, the elbow joint is effectively a hinge joint and it is capable of flexion/extension. Flexion is limited by the size of the biceps and **supinator brevis** which press against each other at the limit of movement. Extension is limited by a bony protuberance from the ulna named the **olecranon process**. As long as movement between these two limits is both full and smooth, then the elbow joint can be said to be flexible.

Ball and socket joints produce a wide range of movement and theoretical maximum flexibility is limited only by such things as the depth of the socket into which the ball joint fits. For practical purposes, flexibility is limited by:

- the tightness of ligaments and the connective tissue capsule which encloses the joint
- the strength of associated muscles and their viscosity
- the tendons through which those muscles act across the joint
- other factors such as feedback mechanisms, muscle size and fatness.

Ligaments respond slightly to training in that their tensile strength builds up. Provided the body is warmed up properly, muscles can be encouraged to relax and to lengthen. In fact, the largest improvement in flexibility comes from relaxing the muscle being stretched.

Large, strong muscles are more difficult to stretch than weaker ones, so training exclusively for muscle strength will reduce flexibility. That is why it is important for strength builders to follow a flexibility programme.

Regular flexibility exercising trains the feedback mechanisms which otherwise cause the muscle we are stretching to contract. This is a self-defence reaction designed to reduce the possibility of injury. It is called the 'myotatic stretch reflex'. Flexibility can be improved by taking a joint to the limit of its movement and holding it there for at least 10 seconds while breathing regularly. Approach the point where discomfort sets in, but do not go beyond it. If movement towards this limit is gradual, the feedback mechanisms in stretching muscles will not cause sudden reflex contraction.

Partners are useful for some flexibility exercises, but they must be careful not to apply too much pressure. Pressure should be applied slowly and progressively until the subject indicates the imminence of discomfort. This should be felt in the belly of the muscle. If it occurs anywhere else, students must stop and examine the way the exercise is being performed.

Jerky movements are less effective for improving flexibility than smooth progression. For example, as the leg is swung upwards, it nears its limit and triggers a myotatic reflex contraction of the stretching hamstrings. This prevents further flexibility. It is, of course, possible to overcome the contraction by using enough force, but this will only cause damage.

Do not yank students' legs apart when they are attempting the splits and do not jerk down on their knees as they stretch thigh adductors.

After an initial period of general flexibility work, target certain joints for specific attention. Do this perhaps half-way through the training session, using it as a natural break between skill acquisition blocs. The body must be thoroughly warmed up. Stretch the targeted muscle as far as sensible and then try to contract it isometrically for up to 10 seconds, before relaxing it and continuing the stretch. In some exercises, it is possible to follow the contraction of the muscle being stretched with a further contraction of those muscles which act in opposition to it. When you have done this for 10 seconds, relax all the muscles and continue into the stretch. These alternative contractions followed by relaxation and further assisted stretching appear to lull the feedback mechanism into accepting further movement at the joint. This is known as 'PNF' stretching, the initials denoting 'Proprioceptive Neuromuscular Facilitation'.

Flexibility is used in a practical sense as a moving or dynamic component of technique performance. The roundhouse kick to the head, for example, flashes up from the ground to head height in such a way as to leave the body in balance as power is transmitted through the trunk and leg muscles.

Lack of flexibility causes a power-wasting, jerky and slow delivery. If the thigh adductors won't stretch sufficiently, the upper body must lean to such an extent that the kick becomes unstable and difficult to retrieve quickly.

The martial artist who has achieved the required degree of suppleness should practise dynamic flexibility exercises related to his techniques. When doing these, he should not attempt to extend the flexibility limits gained through progressive stretching exercises. In my opinion, dynamic flexibility training (sometimes referred to as 'ballistic training') does not replace progressive stretching as a means of safely obtaining improvements.

Questions

1 Why is it necessary to train the joints of the body?
2 What are the two components of joint training?
3 How do they affect joint operation?
4 Is it a good idea to develop these two components separately?
5 How do you avoid over-stressing the joint during training?
6 What are the 5 regions of the spine?
7 What movement is the spine capable of?
8 What kind of joint is the shoulder?
9 What movement is it capable of?
10 How can punching hard without resistance cause elbow damage, and how can this be prevented?
11 What movement are the following joints capable of:
   a the elbow?
   b the wrist?
   c the fingers?
12 What sort of joint is found at the hip?
13 What movement is the hip capable of?
14 What sort of joint is found at the knee?
15 What holds it together?
16 How can it most easily be damaged?
17 What movement is the knee capable of?
18 What sort of joint is found at the ankle?
19 What movement is it capable of?
20 What sort of movement is found at the toes?
21 How does aerobic training affect the heart?

22 What is the desired heart rate for a 30-year-old fit martial artist undergoing aerobic fitness training?

23 Why is it never advisable to stop hard training abruptly?

24 What is the maximum heart rate that a 30-year-old martial artist can safely sustain?

25 What is the vascular shunt?

26 What effect does training have on the volume of oxygen carried in the blood?

27 What effect does training have on the volume of blood in the body?

28 What effect does training have on the capillaries?

29 What effect does training have on the lungs?

30 How does smoking adversely affect training?

31 How does training affect the muscle fibres?

32 Name the 3 types of muscle fibres.

33 Name 2 types of anaerobic respiration.

34 How does training improve them?

35 Why should all rest periods be active?

36 What do the following words mean: isometric, isotonic, concentric and eccentric contraction?

37 What is plyometrics?

38 What are the various ways in which 'strength' can be defined?

39 Compare the differences in general weight training for maximum strength development as opposed to speed/strength.

40 What factors limit movement at a ball-joint?

41 What effect does jerking have on a stretched muscle?

42 Explain the sequence of action in a particular PNF stretch of your choice.

PRACTICAL JOINT STRENGTHENING EXERCISES

As I have already mentioned, strengthening the joints is the first priority of fitness training for *all* martial artists!

The coach must ensure that joint strengthening exercises are performed together with those which promote flexibility. The class must do at least 5 repetitions of 3 sets for each exercise, and students suffering from an injured joint must be encouraged to do even more. Having said that, force may be applied across a damaged joint only on medical advice. In such cases, the coach must advise the student how to strengthen the muscles associated with the joint, without moving the joint itself. All muscles associated with the joint should be exercised equally and each limb must receive the same amount of attention.

I recommend a 'Bullworker' apparatus for strengthening the muscles helping to hold joints together. These are very versatile and can be bought from most sports shops. A medicine ball is also useful. Some traditional training forms are very good for developing isometric strength. I am referring here to such karate katas as **Sanchin**, during which sets of muscles are worked against each other.

Since the strengthening effect of isometric training is very specific, the coach must advise the class to vary the joint angles over which force is applied. Maximum effort should be sustained for around 6 seconds.

The spine

1 *Sacro-iliac*

One of the best exercises for the sacro-iliac is the following traditional Okinawan training method. Though it may seem more than a little odd, it is very effective. The class adopts an hourglass stance (*see photograph 81*). Tell students to keep their backs straight and their knees well bent. The feet are turned inwards. The cheeks of the bottom must be tightly clenched together, so that the hips are lifted up and forwards. On the command, the class advances into a new stance, swinging their rear foot through an arc. Muscular tension must be maintained throughout.

2 *Spinal flexion*

Students are directed to hold a weight that they can easily manage – such as a

81. Exercising the sacro–iliac joint by using the hourglass stance

82. Spinal flexion by dangling the arms in front of the body while holding a medicine ball

83. Spinal extension

84. Spinal lateral flexion

medicine ball – in their arms and lean forwards. Their arms must dangle in front (*see photograph 82*). This position is held for at least 10 seconds whilst breathing easily; then allow students to return to an upright position.

3 *Spinal extension*

Ask the class to put their left leg in front of the right and place their hands on their hips. Then they push their hips forwards and lean well back (*see photograph 83*). This position is held for 10 seconds; then it is followed by an unweighted spinal flexion. On the command, the class returns to a spinal extension, but this time with their right leg forwards.

Alternatively, make the class lie on their front and clasp their hands in the small of their back. Ask them to arch their back and try to raise their chest and knees from the ground. Make them hold this position for up to 10 seconds before relaxing back.

4 *Spinal lateral flexion*

Ask the class to stand with their feet a shoulder-width apart and then lean to the left. Let their left arm lie along their left thigh and bring their right arm over the top of their head (*see photograph 84*). Make them hold this stance for 10 seconds; then change sides. They must work smoothly and not jerk from stance to stance. Alternatively, they can hold medicine balls, or light weights, above their head as they lean from side to side (*see photograph 85*).

85. Flexing the spine laterally by leaning to the side and holding a medicine ball above the head

86. Spinal rotation – look behind you

87. Spinal circumduction by moving the spine in a wide circle

88. Forcing the head backwards against hand pressure to exercise the neck

5 *Spinal rotation*

Tell the students to stand with feet apart and elbows bent. On the command, they must turn their trunk as far as it will go (*see photograph 86*) and hold that position for at least 10 seconds before returning. Then they rotate their bodies in the opposite direction.

6 *Spinal circumduction*

Advise students to avoid strenuous spinal circumduction exercises if they lack flexibility in the spine.

The students must stand with feet apart, holding medicine balls or manageable weights in their outstretched arms. On the command, they move their trunks slowly in a wide circle (*see photograph 87*). When they return to the starting point, they reverse the direction of motion.

7 *Neck exercises*

Use those relevant exercises given in the warm-up sequence on page 66 and, in addition, do the following.

Ask the class to lace their fingers behind their head and try to force their head backwards against the pressure of their hands (*see photograph 88*). Pressure is applied for 10 seconds before relaxing. Then they press both palms against their forehead, whilst resisting. Pressure must be applied for 10 seconds. Finally, tell them to put one hand at the side of their head and apply pressure for 10 seconds whilst resisting (*see photograph 89*). Then they change hands.

89. Pressing the side of the head into a resisting palm

The shoulder

1 *Shoulder flexion*

The students must straighten their elbows and hold a manageable weight in one hand. They raise the weighted arms slowly from their hips to above their heads, pausing in the mid-way position with palms downwards-facing for a count of 10 seconds (*see photograph 90*).

Alternatively, if any student has a damaged shoulder joint, tell him to hook his hand under a solidly fixed shelf and press up against the shelf for a count of 10 seconds.

2 *Shoulder extension*

The students grasp their fingers together behind their neck and tug firmly (*see photograph 91*). Heavily muscled martial artists may not be able to do this, and in such cases a belt grasped in the hands may be used.

Alternatively, students take up a prone, face-down position. Their arms are straightened above their head, with wrists close together. Tell them to press downwards with their palms, as though to lift their upper body from the floor (*see photograph 92*).

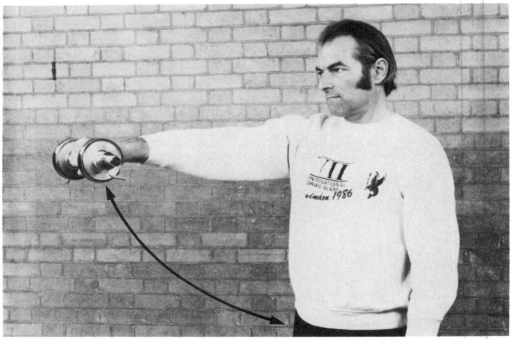

90. Using a weight to flex the right shoulder

91. Shoulder extension

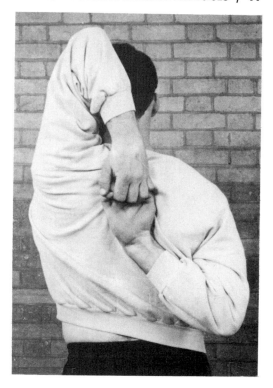

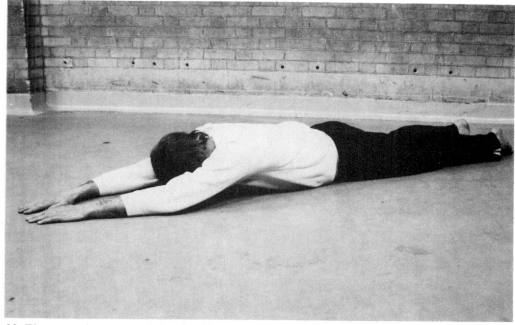

92. Floor exercise to extend the shoulders

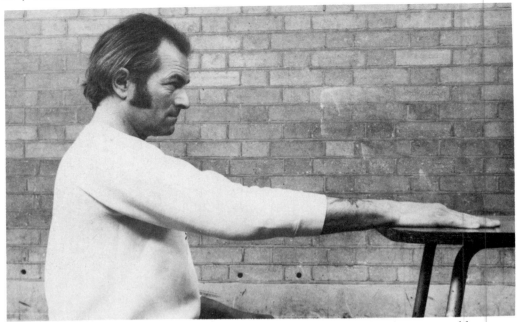

93. During injury, students can practise shoulder extension by pressing down on a table, relaxing, and repeating this exercise several times

Martial artists with shoulder injuries should be advised to straighten their elbows and lay their hands palm-down on a high table, cupboard or shelf. They press downwards for 10 seconds, then relax (*see photograph 93*). Supports of differing height should be used during successive sets of repetitions.

3 *Shoulder horizontal flexion*

The students lie face downwards, their arms extended straight out on either side, palms pressing against the floor. Ask them to press down strongly with their palms, as though to raise their chest from the ground (*see photograph 94*).

94. Horizontal flexion of the shoulder

95. Shoulder flexion using a vertical surface

Alternatively, they may extend their elbows and place their palms against a vertical surface. They apply pressure to their palms for 10 seconds and then relax (*see photograph 95*). Body angle must be altered between successive sets of repetitions.

4 *Shoulder horizontal extension*

The class rolls onto their backs, with their arms straight out and to the sides. Their palms should be facing upwards. See that they keep their elbows rigid and ask them to press down with the backs of their arms against the floor, as though trying to lever themselves up (*see photograph 96*).

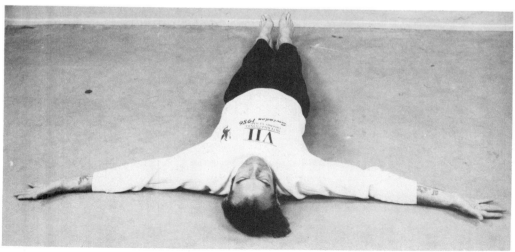

96. Floor exercise to extend the shoulders

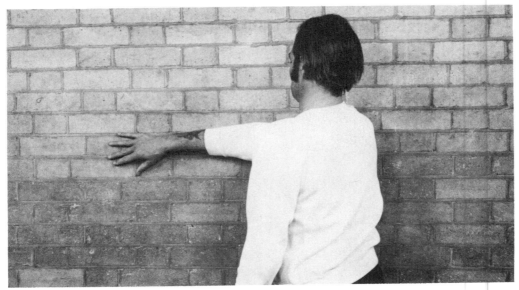

97. Shoulder extension using a vertical surface

Alternatively, students may stand at an acute angle to a vertical surface and turn their palms so that the thumbs face downwards. Tell them to push outwards with their straightened arm for 10 seconds and then to relax it (*see photograph 97*). Make sure they alter the angle of application between successive repetitions.

5 *Shoulder abduction*

The students link their fingers together in front of their stomach and then try to drag their fingers apart. Vary the exercise by making them raise and lower the height of their arms as they are applying pressure (*see photograph 98*).
Alternatively, they may stand sideways-on to a firm shelf or ledge. Tell them to straighten their arms and turn them so the palms face upwards. They must lift their palms to the undersurface of the shelf and apply pressure for 10 seconds. When repeating this exercise, shelves of varying heights should be used.

6 *Shoulder adduction*

Students raise both arms above their heads and bring them together, back to back. They interlace their fingers and then try to pull their arms apart (*see photograph 99*).
Alternatively, a martial artist can stand between two tables, cupboards or filing cabinets and place his straightened arms palm-downwards on them. He presses down firmly with both arms, as though trying to lift his body. If possible, the height of the supports should be varied between successive exercise sets. If only one support is available, tell him to exercise one shoulder joint at a time.

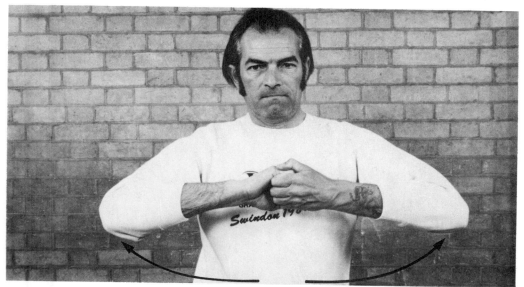

98. Shoulder abduction by linking fingers and trying to pull them apart. Begin at groin height and do not raise elbows above height of chest

99. Shoulder adduction

100. Shoulder circumduction whilst resisting the movement

7 Shoulder circumduction

Students take their right wrist in their left hand and move their straightened right arm in a wide circle, all the time resisting strongly with the left (*see photograph 100*). They reverse the direction of circling and then change arms.

8 Shoulder external rotation

Students flex their right elbow joint and grasp their wrist in their left hand. They should keep the forearm horizontal at stomach height and should try to move it away from the stomach whilst strongly resisting with their left hand (*see photograph 101*). They change arms after a number of repetitions.

9 Shoulder internal rotation

Students bend their right arms as before and make a hammer fist, with the palm pointing upwards. The little finger edge of the fist must be located against the palm of their left hand. They push inwards with their fist, resisting with their palm (*see photograph 102*). The forearm must be kept horizontal.

101. Internal rotation of the right shoulder pulling the right wrist outwards

102. Internal rotation of the right shoulder pushing the right fist inwards

The elbow

1 *Elbow flexion*

The students place their palms together on the side of their body, the left on top of the right. They keep their right elbow close to their side and attempt to lift their right palm whilst resisting strongly with the left (*see photograph 103*). This exercise should be repeated several times before changing the arm over.

2 *Elbow extension*

The students bend their right arm, bringing the fist close to their shoulder. They bring their left arm across and place the palm against the back of their right wrist. The fist is pushed downwards whilst resisting with the left hand (*see photograph 104*).

103. Elbow flexion by pushing up the right hand against resistance

104. Elbow extension by pushing down the right hand

3 Elbow pronation and supination

The students bend their elbows and grip a firmly mounted bar in an over-hand grasp. They must try to rotate their forearms as though turning their fists, palms upward-facing (*see photograph 105*). Torsion is applied for 10 seconds, followed by relaxation and further repetitions. Next they grip the bar with an under-hand grasp and try to rotate their fists palm downward-facing (*see photograph 106*). Coaches should not use the exercise which winds a weight up by pronation/supination (*see photograph 107*). This can cause tennis or golfers' elbow.

The wrist

1 Wrist flexion

Students bend their elbows and make a fist close to their chest with their right hand. They extend the wrist joint and cup the bent fingers in a left palm-heel (*see photograph 108*). The wrist joint is then flexed against the palm-heel, ensuring that the latter grudgingly yields.

2 Wrist extension

Students next fully flex their wrist joints in the above configuration and bring their

105. Over-hand grasp of the bar

106. Under-hand grasp of the bar

107. This exercise should be avoided, since it can cause injury to the elbow

Below left 108. Wrist flexion by forcing the palm against the left hand

Below right 109. Wrist extension against pressure

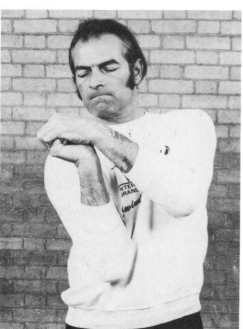

110. Resisting movement of the wrist from side to side

left hand over the backs of the knuckles (*see photograph 109*). They then try to extend their wrists against resistance from the left hand.

3 *Wrist side-to-side*

In this exercise, students extend their fingers and turn their right hand so the palm faces the ground. The fingers are held in an over-hand grasp with their left hand. Students then try to move their wrist from side to side whilst resisting with their left hand (*see photograph 110*).

The fingers and thumbs

One of the best finger and thumb exercisers is an elastic web that has meshes large enough through which to insert fingers. This is available through martial art shops and can be used for strengthening all finger and thumb functions.

1 *Finger flexion*

The class can use a finger flexion exerciser bought from general sports shops. This consists of a 'v' spring squeezed between the palm and the fingers as they flex. As an alternative, students can roll their fingers around a fat length of tube and squeeze it hard.

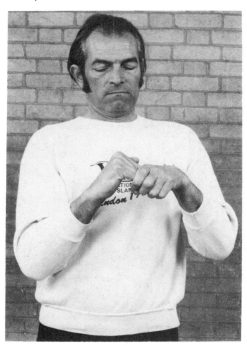

111. Finger extension against resistance

2 *Finger extension*

Students can use the training web, selecting holes which are close together. They try to force the web to open.

Alternatively, they can roll their fingers into the palm of their other hand and push against them (*see photograph 111*).

3 *Thumb opposition*

A combination of opposition and finger flexion produces grip. The elastic web can be used to develop grip, or students can simply squeeze a solid ball (about the size of a tennis ball) in their hands. Alternatively, they can grip a fat tube and squeeze hard.

The hip

1 *Hip flexion*

Weighted sandals are useful for strengthening hip flexors. Students should load them to a manageable level and slowly and smoothly lift their feet until the knees approach their chests. There is a 10-second pause at the mid-way point.

If the coach doesn't have access to weighted sandals, an elastic luggage strap with

112. Hip flexion, using a partner to resist raising of the right knee

hooks at either end can be used. This must be firmly secured; then the student hooks his foot under it and lifts.

Alternatively, divide the class in half, with one group on their backs with knees lifted. The other half of the class acts as partners, sitting in front and lacing their fingers over the top of the lifted knees. As the active students try to lift their knees further towards themselves, their partners resist (*see photograph 112*).

2 *Hip extension*

Students stand with their backs against a wall, their feet a shoulder-width apart and turned slightly outwards. They gradually slide down the wall and allow their knees to flex until there is a ninety degree angle between their upper and lower legs (*see photograph 113 overleaf*). This position is held for as long as possible.

3 *Hip abduction*

Students lie on their left side and brace themselves. On the command, they raise their right leg smoothly to an angle of around 30 degrees from the horizontal (*see photograph 114 overleaf*) and hold them there for a count of 10. Both legs should be exercised equally.

113. Hip extension using gravity

114. Hip abduction, holding the raised leg to an angle of about 30°

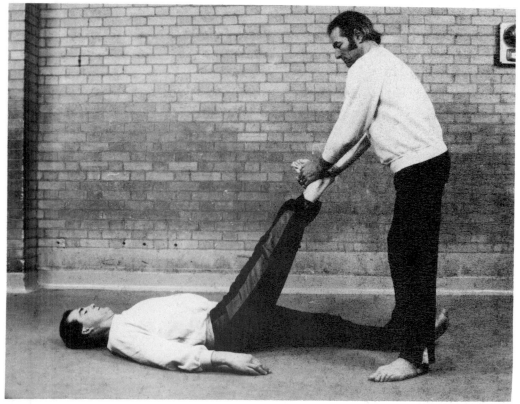

115. Hip circumduction, working against resistance offered by a partner

4 *Hip adduction*

A good exercise for the thigh adductors uses a medicine ball. If no medicine ball is available, then another suitable object can be used. The class should sit down and place the medicine ball between their knees. They squeeze their knees together for a count of 10 seconds and then relax.

5 *Hip circumduction*

This exercise requires partners. One student lies on his back and offers his straightened leg to the partner. The latter should feel the movement of the leg and should resist it (*see photograph 115*).

6 *Hip internal and external rotation*

Students with knee problems should not perform this exercise! It also requires partners. One student lies on his back and offers a straightened leg to his partner. He then attempts to rotate his hip against moderate resistance (*see photograph 116*).

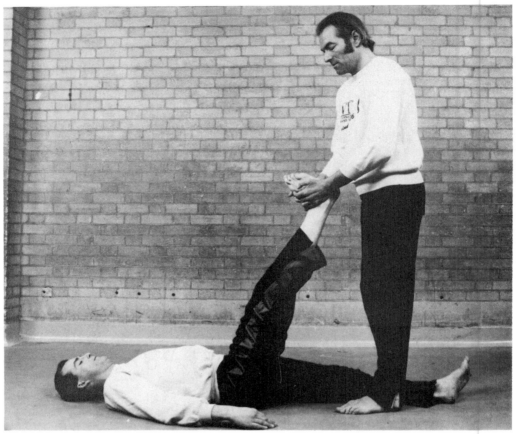

116. Internal and external rotation of the hip. Don't try this if you have bad knees!

The knee

1 *Knee flexion and extension*

This exercise is performed from a prone position. Students lie on their backs and each lifts a straight leg to an angle of around 30 degrees from the horizontal (*see photograph 117*). This is held for 10 seconds and is then slowly lowered to the floor. The exercise is repeated a number of times on both legs.

As an individual exercise, the student can take up a sitting position, hooking his heel in front of a secure step. The hips are anchored by holding to the underneath of a chair. The student tries to drag his heel back (*see photograph 118*), holding the muscle contraction for 10 seconds. A number of repetitions are performed.

As a continuation of the last exercise, the student should next try to extend his leg against the step, thereby contracting the muscles on the front of his thigh.

117. Straight leg lifts flex and extend the right knee from a prone position

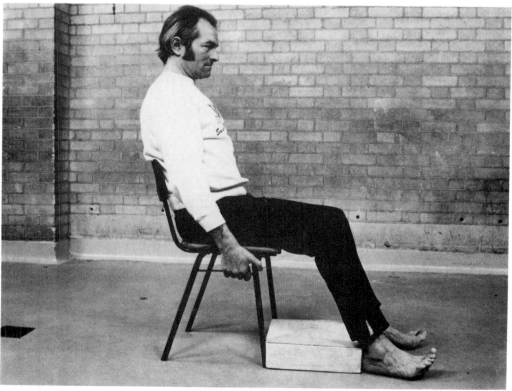

118. Flexion of the knees from a seated position

The ankle

All ankle movement can be strengthened by a wobble-board. This is a circle of thick plywood with a wooden hemisphere on one side. The student stands on the flat surface of the board and tries to keep his balance. As he becomes able to do this, his partner gently throws a medicine ball to him. This must be caught and returned whilst he remains in balance on the board.

1 *Plantar flexion*

Students stand upright and raise their heels clear of the floor (*see photograph 119*). This position should be held for at least 10 seconds before relaxing back. The exercise should be repeated a number of times.

Walking on tiptoe is another good exercise for strengthening plantar flexion.

2 *Dorsi-flexion*

Students stand with their heels overlapping a step. On the command, they lower their heels below the level of the step. This position is held for 10 seconds and then the exercise is repeated.

3 *Ankle eversion, inversion and circumduction*

These exercises are performed from a sitting position. Students cross their right leg over their left leg, then take their ankle in their left hand and resist the movement as they successively evert, invert and circumduct the joint (*see photograph 120*).

119. Plantar flexion by raising the heels off the floor against gravity

120. Taking the ankle through its full range of movement from a sitting position

Toes

1 Toe flexion and extension

Students pull their toes back as far as they will go, holding the position for at least 10 seconds (*see photograph 121*). The coach must note that it is all too easy to over-train the **peroneal** muscle during toe flexion exercises. The outcome of this ('Anterior Compartment Syndrome') is quite unpleasant and requires surgical intervention.

Students next turn their toes downwards for as long as they can without getting cramp. Alternatively, they may practise picking up matchboxes with their toes.

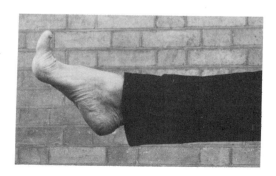

121. Flexion of the toes during front kicks

PRACTICAL BODY PREPARATION EXERCISES

This is the second priority of fitness training. Whereas the warm-up aims to bring the body into a state where it moves freely and effectively within its normal limits, body preparation seeks to extend those limits.

Endurance

Aerobic

The object of aerobic training is to work steadily for 20 or 30 minutes, repeated 3 or 4 times a week. As a guide for determining the sustained heart rate where aerobic effect occurs, use the following formula:

$$220 - (martial\ artist's\ age + 25)$$

or refer to the following table:

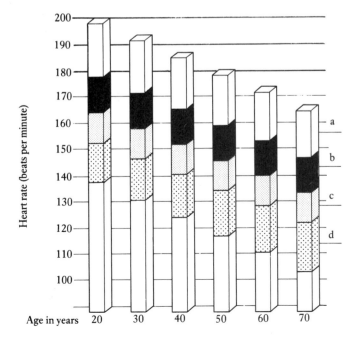

Table 1

116

If this heart rate cannot be sustained for the full period, lighten the exercise until it can. Monitor students' progress and increase exercise rate until the highest continuous (and safe) heart rate can be sustained for the session.

As students become more aerobically fit, extend the duration of training. Then increase the workload so the heart rate rises, thus improving heart and lung operation. As work load increases, students may experience difficulty in lasting the extended training period. If this happens, reduce the exercise load until the pulse drops back to around 120 beats per minute, and then step it back up again.

Fitter students will only need a short rest because their heart rate quickly drops. Take fully fit students right up to the anaerobic threshold and then drop them back before returning to a still higher workload. This form of interval training is extremely effective.

Many exercises can be used. Jogging or running are fine, but warn against doing a lot of work on hard roads. This does the joints little good. Overweight students may also find that jogging aggravates back problems. Cycling can be used as a very effective aerobic training exercise, as can swimming – though different people react differently to each.

Try to match the exercise to the martial art. Explain to students what it is you want them to achieve and perhaps launch into combination technique practice. Set the kitchen timer for 25 minutes and work the class smoothly and continuously, mixing a wide variety of techniques and allowing no respite. Instruct the students to pace themselves so that their heart rate enters and remains within the training band for the full training period. Ensure that their arms and legs are used equally.

Mirror sparring is an effective means of individually training aerobically. Students work out in front of a mirror that gives a full-length reflection. They maintain a constant level of activity, mixing punches and kicks with blocks and body movements. They work at all times within the aerobic band.

Use slowed-down free sparring for more experienced classes, but ensure everyone is well padded. Despite the lower speed, injuries do still occur. Observe one strict protocol: if someone delivers a slowed down kick, the opponent must not seize hold of it.

Kata/poomse/patterns are also good for building aerobic endurance in experienced classes. Raise the speed of technique delivery so there are few hesitations and an overall smooth execution from beginning to end. Taekwondo poomse are particularly suitable for this, whereas correctly performed **shorei** karate katas are not. Either repeat one form or take the class through a whole series. Allow no rests between performances. This form of body preparation is more interesting than just performing exercises and it has the added advantage of improving skills.

Anaerobic – phosphagen system

This training is characterised by bursts of maximum effort separated by active rest periods. Explain how training operates, so students understand that they must literally work explosively for 15/20 seconds.

Use short sprints of up to 50 metres, separated by jogging for 2 minutes. The coach carries a stopwatch and suddenly shouts 'Go!', and away sprint the students. 15 seconds later, he calls 'Stop!' and everyone drops to a jog.

Repeat this over a period of 10 minutes and then allow a 10-minute rest period. Walk the students for part of this longer rest period. Then take them into gentle stretching exercises.

Select martial art techniques for more experienced students. Have students deliver a sustained barrage of full power hand techniques into a punchbag for 15 seconds. Reduce down to light impacts and then shoot back up to maximum effort, but this time use kick techniques. Alternate between kicks and punches. Give rests as per the short sprint drill outlined above.

As the session continues, you can gradually lower the active unit to perhaps 80% of maximum, but allow only eight units of rest.

Anaerobic – glycolysis

The glycolysis system needs near maximum effort to engage, so training should be hard, with intervals of lighter work acting as active rest periods. Measure the students' maximum performances in a particular exercise over perhaps 60 seconds. Use running, step-ups onto a bench, press-ups, or martial art techniques and count the number of repetitions made in that minute.

Let's suppose that student Fred can do a maximum of 60 press-ups in 60 seconds. In this case, set Fred the task of doing 45 press-ups in a minute. When he finishes, let him rest actively for 2 minutes by doing some light punch training against a target mitt. At the end of the rest, have Fred turn in another 45 press-ups, and so on until training has gone on for about 12 minutes.

Measure the number of press-ups Fred does in each of six 10-second segments making up one set. This is useful for showing the onset of fatigue.

When Fred can manage the task, increase his workload to 50 press-ups per minute. As his ability to tolerate lactic acid build-up improves, cut rest intervals progressively from 1 minute to 30 seconds. When Fred reaches this stage, he is engaging his glycolytic system and is mobilising the fast twitch white fibres that he will need in his competition bout.

Those martial artists who engage in single bout competition can have their workloads extended to 2 minutes, with a 4-minute active rest dropping eventually to only 1 minute between sets.

When setting work and rest intervals in élite performers, the coach must decide whether they are naturally fast performers with a high proportion of fast twitch white fibres, or whether they are not so much fast as tactical. Those with lots of white fibres will produce large volumes of lactic acid, so to stimulate the removal system their work periods can be shortened in relationship to the rest intervals. Those who are maybe not as fast may have a lower proportion of white fibres and so must work harder for longer periods to produce more lactic acid. This is improved by shorter rest intervals.

Strength

Three general strength sessions per week are required for the average martial artist. Each session should be not less than 30 minutes and no longer than 1 hour in duration. They must be interspersed with days of rest.

Arrange each session to work the stronger leg muscles first, followed by the arms and the abdominals. Students perform one exercise in each of these groups, then do a second and different exercise for each. The desired strength level is maintained by one session per week.

Weight training

The following precautions must be taken when using weights to develop strength:

- a thorough warm-up must precede all weight training
- exercises should work a joint through its entire safe range of movement
- exercises must not be damaging to joints. Do not drop into a full squat – a half-squat is sufficient. When taking weight on the shoulders, do not curve the spine
- increase in loading should be gradual. Female martial artists will require a more gradual increase than their male counterparts
- vary the exercises to get the best effect
- stop if pain is felt in the muscle being exercised
- do not follow a hard weight training session with other hard work
- insert rest days between weight training sessions.

The following general weight training exercises may be of interest.

The half squat The student stands upright with the bar across his shoulders and behind his neck. He sinks down to a half-squat position (*see photograph 122 overleaf*), pauses slightly and then drives upright once more. He should not bounce back up, or drop too low.

The bicep curl The student stands upright with the bar across the front of his thighs. He flexes his elbows and raises the bar (*see photograph 123 overleaf*) until it reaches his chest. After a pause, he lowers it slowly and smoothly back. He should not use his hips to spring the bar up.

The sit-up The student lies on his back with his knees bent. He holds a weight behind his head with both hands. He lifts his shoulders and upper back clear of the floor (*see photograph 124 overleaf*), pauses and then slowly returns. He should not bounce down and straight back up again. The training effect can be varied by twisting the trunk as he raises up, first to one side, then the other. Novices will find it easier to 'cuddle' the weight against their chests.

122. The half squat

123. Raising the bar during the biceps curl

124. Performing a sit-up, with a weight held behind the head

The clean The student squats with a straight back whilst holding the bar. He fully straightens his legs and brings the bar past the front of his thighs. As it reaches his shoulders, he bends his knees and drops under it. He straightens his legs and holds the bar in a palm-upwards hold (*see photograph 125*). The return is smooth and controlled. At no time should he curve his back.

125. Holding position of the clean lift

126. Starting position for the back squat lift

The back squat (also called **the back lift**) The student squats down with a straight back, the bar behind his heels (*see photograph 126*). He stands up, straightening his legs smoothly. Then he makes a controlled return back into the squat. He should not bounce down and back up again.

127. Maximum upward extension of the bench press

128. Jump squat while holding the bar in front of the body

The bench press The student lies on his back, with the bar across his chest and elbows bent. He smoothly pushes the bar upwards until his elbows lock straight (*see photograph 127*). Then he lowers it back gently, pauses, and pushes it up again. The training effect is varied by narrowing and widening the grip on the bar.

Jump squats This is performed as for half-squats above, but as he straightens, the student jumps clear of the ground (*see photograph 128*). He bends his knees on landing and carefully lowers himself back into a half-squat once again. He should not bounce down after landing.

Straight-leg deadlift The student bends both knees and grasps the bar which is on the floor in front of him. He straightens his knees and lifts the bar so that it hangs in front of his thighs.

Upright rowing The student grasps the bar in an overhand manner, with thumbs close together. It hangs down in front of his thighs and he raises it by bringing his elbows up (*see photograph 129*). The bar is held for an instant and is then lowered smoothly. If the student has a strong back, he may lean forwards and let the bar hang. He then performs bent-over rowing (*see photograph 130*).

Split squats The student begins from a long stance, holding the bar across the back of his neck. He jumps up and changes legs in mid-air, returning to a new long stance.

129. Upright rowing exercise

130. Bent-over rowing exercise

131. Starting position for the French press

Military press The student holds the bar across the front of his chest and presses it firmly upwards, until his elbows lock straight. He holds it there for a short time and then slowly lowers it back to his chest. The exercise is varied by resting the bar on the back of the neck and pressing up from there.

Calf raise The student rests the bar across his shoulders and behind his neck. His feet should be hip-width apart, with his toes turned slightly outwards. He raises his heels clear of the floor, pauses and then slowly lowers them back down.

French press The student rests the bar across his shoulders and behind his neck. His elbows are raised and are bent (*see photograph 131*). He extends his elbows until they lock out straight (*see photograph 132*), pauses there, and then returns the bar to his shoulders once more.

Straight arm pull-over The student lies in a bench press position, with the bar held on straight arms. He keeps his arms straight as he gradually lowers the bar (*see photograph 133*). Then he slowly returns it to the start position once more.

132. Maximum upward extension of the French press

133. Lowering the bar during the straight arm pull-over

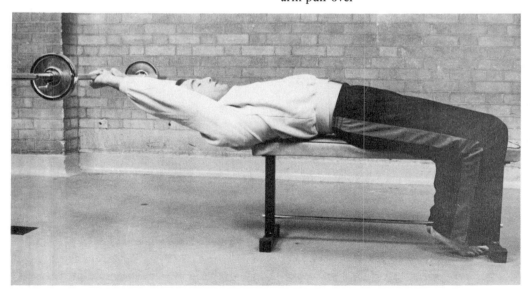

Begin weight training by determining students' present strength level. Measure maximum performances and make a note of them. For example, if Freda can curl a maximum of 25 kilogrammes, then make her curl $12\frac{1}{2}$ kilos 10 times. She should rest for 2 minutes and continue with 5 repetitions at 18 kilos. Allow another rest, and, finally, put 24 kilos on the bar and make her lift it once. This is the principle of 'pyramid training'.

Alternatively, find out the maximum weight Freda can lift 10 times. Then make Freda lift half of that weight for 10 repetitions. Give a 2-minute rest and increase the weight to three-quarters for a second set of 10 repetitions. Lastly, increase to the original load and let her perform a final set of 10 repetitions. Encourage Freda to try to exceed the 10 repetition maximum load; as soon as she can, the series should be recalibrated.

To develop Freda's strength, make her lift $12\frac{1}{2}$ kilos in 6 repetitions. Go on to other exercises, returning shortly afterwards to your second set of 6 repetitions. After a similar rest interval, return for a third set. As Freda becomes able to tolerate this level of work, increase weight to a maximum of 20 kilos.

To develop Freda's strength/speed, make her curl only 6 kilos, raising the bar as quickly as possible each time for 20 repetitions. If Freda easily manages this, maintain the weight but increase the number of repetitions. Use a stop-watch to see how long it takes her. You can also use your stop-watch to see how many curls she can perform in 20/30 seconds. However, do not let the quality of the exercise be sacrificed to speed.

The difference is therefore obvious. Building strength requires heavy weights moved over only a few consecutive repetitions. Building strength/speed needs light weights moved quickly over a high number of repetitions.

Useful short-range strength/speed for martial arts can be developed in a number of ways. One involves using a medicine ball. Freda stands in an upright stance, holding the medicine ball in both hands, with her elbows slightly bent. She throws the ball as far as possible using a spasm action of her upper body muscles (*see photograph 134*). The trunk may move slightly during this drill. The ball is returned by a resting student.

Freda performs 3 sets of 20 throws and then acts as ball-catcher for her partner during the rest period. Reduce the number of repetitions for students with weak musculature.

The second drill uses specialised equipment, so I am mentioning it only for your interest. It consists of a pulley frame bolted to the wall of the training room. When one of the two D-rings is pulled or pushed forwards, weights are raised from the floor. The special adaptation I am referring to is the low power take-off. In normal frames, this is at shoulder height, but in George Andrew's variant it is at waist height.

George uses the frame to develop a particular type of stance stability. If you don't get it right, you have to lean forwards – and this is regarded as a fault. It occurred to me that by reducing the weight pullied up each time and by increasing the speed,

134. Using muscle spasm to throw a medicine ball

this might prove useful for developing those short-distance punches that drive off the hip.

Martial arts which use throws can develop specific strength and speed/strength by means of springs or inner tubes securely attached to wallbars. A mannequin with pre-bent arms and legs could prove very effective if weighted correctly for practice. Free-standing rugby tackle bags might be worth trying.

Heavier than standard martial arts weapons will develop the forearms and upper body musculature.

Bodyweight strength exercises

These exercises use only the weight of the body to produce a training effect. Consider the following.

Press-ups Refer to pages 48–51 for a description of the various forms of press-up. Regular press-ups which make use of an explosive action are better for developing power. Inclined press-ups (*see photograph 135 overleaf*) will increase strength.

Squats These are performed as for the free weight exercise. The student drops into a half squat and pushes up explosively. Striking-based martial artists can perform alternate leg kicks as they straighten up (*see photograph 136 overleaf*).

135. Inclined press-ups increase strength

136. Straightening up from a squat and kicking

137. Using strong, stable chairs for performing dips

Abdominal crunches The student lies on his back and bends his knees. He brings his heels close to his bottom. Then he pulls his upper body off the ground, holds, and relaxes back.

Dips The student braces himself on straight arms between parallel bars. Gradually he lowers his body by bending his elbows. He pauses at the lowest point, then pushes himself back up. He should not bounce down and back up in one movement. If you have no access to parallel bars, a pair of strong and stable chairs can be used (*see photograph 137*). The exercise can also be performed using just one chair.

Split squats These are performed as for the free-weight exercise. The student uses a very long and low stance, but he does not bend his knees past 90 degrees at any time. He springs high into the air and changes his stance upon landing.

Inclined sit-ups Refer to pages 53–4 for sit-up exercises. Increases in strength can be obtained if the student lies back on an inclined board. He should not let his legs extend (*see photograph 138 overleaf*).

Chins The student grasps a horizontal bar with an underhand grip and hangs suspended. He smoothly pulls himself up until his chin is level with the top of the

138. Inclined sit-ups build abdominal
strength, but do not let the legs extend. This
can injure the back

139. Grasp the bar, with an underhand grip,
and pull up until you literally 'chin' the bar

bar (*see photograph 139*). He holds this position and then lowers back down in a controlled manner. He should not immediately bounce back up again. The exercise may be varied by changing to an overhand grasp.

140. Starting position of a reverse punch, with hips turned 45° away

141. Driving down the ball of the right foot and rotating the hips

Plyometrics

This harnesses the fast, involuntary contraction which follows an evoked stretch reflex. There are no specific martial art drills for utilising this and the following suggestions are for discussion purposes only:

a   The student practises a reverse punch from a medium-length left stance. His front foot faces forwards and his back leg is rotated 45 degrees from straight ahead. His left arm is held well forwards and his right arm is bent at the elbow and held well back from the body (*see photograph 140 on previous page*). If the coach looks carefully, he will see that the student's hips are facing 45 degrees off from ahead.

142. Release the reverse punch as maximum hip rotation is marked

On the command, the student drives down with the ball of his foot and rotates his hips so that they begin to turn forwards. He should not allow his shoulders and arms to change from the starting position (*see photograph 141*). As he does this, he will feel a strain in his **pectoralis major, obliquus** and **serratus magnus** muscles as they are stretched. Tension will continue to rise as the hips further rotate and, as this reaches a peak, he releases the punch and contracts the above muscles as quickly as he can (*see photograph 142*).

The rotation of the hips which stretches the muscles must be made as quickly as possible and the punch itself must release at the optimum time. The student must try to throw as many punches as he can for 30 seconds, before changing arms and repeating the exercise. The second set should last 15 seconds, with a 30-second rest, and the final set should be of 10 seconds' duration.

143. One-legged bounds alternately flex . . .

144. . . . and extend the knee joints, working the muscles plyometrically

b   The student performs 3 sets of one-legged bounds that zig-zag. He lands with a bent knee, letting it yield under him before springing up and across in the other direction (*see photographs 143 and 144*). At no time should the knee bend more than 90 degrees. The first set operates for 30 seconds at half-speed and is followed by a 30-second active rest. The second set operates at three-quarters speed for 15 seconds. After a further half minute, the final set operates at maximum speed for 10 seconds.

Now make up your own specific drills and let me know how you get on!

Speed

As I mentioned earlier, there are no specific martial art speed drills, though I have suggested some ways in which particular techniques might be made faster. The following may help you to visualise the sort of training needed. The first is a general speed drill to try when the muscles are loose through a good warm-up or through previous *light* training.

a   Running on the spot. Students must fetch their knees up as high as they can and work their arms violently. Aim for flat out activity lasting 10 seconds; then give a full recovery. Repeat the drill twice more, with perhaps some gentle stretching or walking around between sets.

b   Have students perform 3 sets of 3 harness sprints of no more than 10 metres each, commencing from a martial art stance. Allow a gentle but active recovery between each. Give a longer rest between sets. Watch the starting stance carefully and encourage any adaptations which seem to give a better spring-off without prejudicing the guard.

c   Use something like a chest expander or long luggage elastic (or tyre innertube), one end of which is firmly attached to the wall. There must be sufficient elasticity to accommodate the whole movement. Trial and error will determine exactly how far the students must stand from the anchorage to allow their punches to extend. They grip the resistance by means of D-rings and punch at full speed, aiming to do as many repetitions as they can for a maximum of 15 seconds. Make them change arms and repeat. Do a total of 3 sets on each arm.

Technique quality is important and must not be sacrificed to speed. Try various types and lengths of stance to see whether they give any worthwhile increase. Design a similar rig for spring-resisted front kicks.

d   Spring-assisted punches work in a similar fashion except that the student faces the spring and draws back his punch against tension. He stands in such a way that the spring pull reaches zero while there is still a slight angle in the elbow. He musn't stand so close that he punches the wall! When he has fully cocked his fist, he drives it forwards and allows the spring to assist the movement. Do not allow the arm to jam straight or he will quickly damage his elbow. Tell the student to perform 20 punches and then to change arms. Design a similar drill for spring-assisted front kicks.

Reaction training

Combine speed work with reaction training. Impact-based martial arts can make good use of the plastazote foam impact pad, or a target mitt. The coach holds this down and suddenly presents it either square-on (*see photograph 145 on page 136*) or side-on (*see photograph 146 on page 137*). It is presented only for a short time and height is varied between head and trunk. Students must react to pad-presentation with a technique appropriate to its height and angle.

Presentation times vary according to the technique used. Allow more time when kick responses are made. When the student is hitting the pad 9 times out of 10, begin to weave it slowly about during presentation. Move forwards and step back to give practice at ranging on moving targets. Disallow techniques with poor form and those which land with either too little or too much force.

Encourage students to use perhaps only four general techniques, so there will be less delay while the brain selects one. As with all work of this type, training must not be fatiguing because reaction time increases as tiredness creeps in.

145. Square-on presentation of the target mitt

Flexibility

General flexibility forms part of the warm-up. Refer to pages 56–63 to refresh your memory. Target specific areas of flexibility relevant to your martial art practice and work on them at a mid-point in the training session. I have never encountered a student whose lack of shoulder flexibility limited his skill training, whereas virtually all students lacked sufficient trunk/hip flexibility. It is for that reason I am going to concentrate on the latter.

By far the majority of students lack the flexibility needed to abduct the thigh sufficiently (*see photograph 147*). This can be improved by stretching the antagonist muscles – the thigh adductors. A lot of students also cannot get sufficient hip flexion. This can be improved by stretching the hamstring muscles.

Work students singly, or in pairs. Take them to the limit of joint movement and hold it there for periods of up to 30 seconds. Students who have trained in flexibility previously may be asked to contract/relax isometrically the muscle being

146. Side-on presentation of the target mitt

147. Abduction of the right thigh

stretched and, where it is possible, the antagonists, too. All muscles are then relaxed for the PNF effect. Perform the following exercises in addition to those in the warm-up section.

Stretch a student's thigh adductors by sitting him down with feet drawn up and knees bent. Use partners for the best effect to press firmly down on his open knees whilst he relaxes (*see photograph 148*). He holds the lowest position for up to 30 seconds and then contracts his adductors, forcing up against the partner's downward push. He holds this contraction for at least 10 seconds before relaxing his adductors once more.

148. Using a partner to stretch the thigh adductors

An alternative method for stretching the adductors in a different way uses gravity. The student lies on his back with his bottom pressed against a wall and his legs extended upwards. He allows his legs to open whilst relaxing his thigh adductors. The weight of his legs gradually stretches the adductors (*see photograph 149*). When discomfort sets in, he simply contracts the adductors and raises his legs slightly against gravity. He relaxes them once more and allows the stretch to resume.

Use partners to help stretch the hamstrings (hip flexion). The student lies on his back and offers his right leg. The partner takes his ankle and pushes his leg upwards. The leg must not bend and the other foot must remain flat on the floor. The **biceps, semitendinosus** and **semimembranosus** muscles on the back of the thigh must be relaxed so that they stretch easily (*see photograph 150*). When the normal limit is reached, the student contracts those same muscles for 10 seconds and then relaxes once more. If he can manage it, he should contract the quadriceps extensors, as though trying to pull the knee towards his face. Finally, he relaxes all muscles and completes the stretch.

149. Using gravity to stretch the thigh adductors

150. Using a partner to stretch the right hamstring. The knee should be kept extended

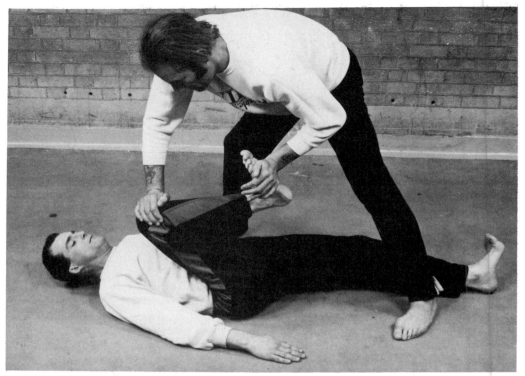

151. Hip flexion flexibility training using a partner to push the knee back

Use this same format to stretch the thigh adductors. The student lies on his side and pulls his foot into a side-kick configuration. He braces himself by spreading his arms.

Vary hip flexion flexibility training by asking the student to bend his knee joint and then allow the partner to press his heel towards his chest (*see photograph 151*). He should contract his muscles against the applied pressure and should then relax once more.

Plantar flexion flexibility can be improved by making the class kneel for increasing periods of time. Cushions under the insteps may help at first. Stretch the quadriceps by making students lean back from this position whilst keeping their toes pointed.

COACHING FOR HEALTH AND SAFETY

Prevention is better than cure!

A major priority for any coach must be to limit the possibility of injury to students during training, and many of the ways of achieving this are covered elsewhere in this book. They can be summarised thus, by:

- screening students to ensure they are fit to practise
- providing coaches who are adequately skilled and properly trained to direct martial art practice
- ensuring that students are properly warmed up before training commences
- preparing students so they are able to meet the physical and mental demands of martial art practice
- training students with exercises, techniques and practice forms which are suitable for their technical standard, physical abilities and age
- avoiding exercises and forms of training which are known to involve risk of injury
- adequately supervising students during all aspects of their practice, and providing them with advice and direction
- monitoring the training of students so they are not overstressed, physically or mentally
- using rules approved by the national (or international) governing bodies for the operation of courses, tournaments and events of whatsoever nature
- providing a training facility, martial art equipment and ancillary items which are safe for usage and which are regularly maintained.

Screening students

Coaches are recommended to use the standard application form shown on page 188. This lists the scheduled health conditions to be declared. Only one is serious enough to preclude training altogether, and that is **haemophilia**. Persons who suffer from a milder variant, known as **Von Willebrandt's Disease**, may be allowed to train with the approval of their doctor.

Cardiac sufferers can be accepted but only after clearance from their doctors. They should be allowed to drop out of training if chest pains are experienced. They must not be encouraged to try to go through the pain barrier!

Martial art training benefits asthma sufferers, though the coach must insist they bring their medication into the training hall. During an intensive session, diabetics may become sugar-starved and may begin to act oddly. The coach should ensure they take lemonade or something similar into the training hall and they should put it in a conspicuous place.

Few people suffer from full-blown epilepsy; most experience only **petit mal** seizures from which a quick recovery is the norm. Sufferers of the more serious variant can train safely if the floor is padded, though coaches must know how to put them into the prone recovery position.

Providing qualified coaches

Qualified coaches make a major contribution to prevention and rehabilitation of injury. In contrast, many untrained teachers have, to my own certain knowledge, actually caused unintentional injury to their students.

Ensuring that students are properly warmed up

The importance of a thorough warm-up is covered more fully elsewhere in this book. Suffice it to say here that the warm-up rehearses the tissues of the body so they are prepared for the demands that training will shortly put upon them. When muscles are warmed up, they are less likely to be injured by sudden and violent movements of the type encountered in martial art practice.

Preparing students to cope with the demands of training

Many martial art techniques require high levels of power and flexibility. High kicks, for example, rely upon a mobile hip joint. If the joint is not flexible enough, injury can occur at the limits of movement. Therefore, before asking the student to perform such techniques, the coach must prepare them. Technique progression introduces the correct movement and body preparation allows the extension of that movement.

Using appropriate exercises and training forms

The child cannot train in the same way that an adult can. His young tissues are still forming and are vulnerable to damage. Particularly susceptible are the growing points of the bones and joints. Training must take this into account.

Students with declared health conditions must be similarly protected and it is part of the coach's duty to determine what special requirements are needed in each case.

Avoiding injurious exercises and training methods

Certain exercises, such as those involving ballistic stretching, give rise to an unacceptable risk of injury. Therefore, they should not be practised. Training methods in which powerful techniques are delivered against zero resistance have been shown to be harmful.

No training of any kind should be permitted until students are capable of performing it safely.

Adequately supervising students

Risk of injury increases in the absence of safe supervision. Therefore, the coach must supervise all activity. Children are particularly at risk.

Monitoring students

The coach assesses the effect his training is having by observing the students. If students are trained too hard, they become fatigued. The general symptoms of fatigue are:

- the student becomes listless and lacks enthusiasm
- he complains of losing his appetite, and he gradually loses weight
- he always seems tired, even before beginning the session
- he quickly falls prey to any infections currently around.

If the coach fails to note the onset of fatigue symptoms, the student's condition worsens and acute signs begin to appear. 'Glandular fever' is not uncommon in such cases. This can be very debilitating and persistent.

Using approved rules

Injuries in a martial art tournament can be reduced by:

- using rules which prohibit excessive contact to the body and any contact to the face and head
- ensuring the application of these rules by properly trained officials
- limiting entry to martial artists with sufficient skill
- matching competitors according to divisions of age, weight, sex, height, etc.

The rules of competition are very important to the safety of participants. They set out what is, and what is not, permitted, so participants are forewarned about what to expect!

Any person who participates under rules which allow heavy and repeated contact to the head will suffer brain damage. This is not as clearly seen as a bloody nose, so people may wrongly assume that no damage is occurring.

Properly trained officials are essential for safe competitions. They understand exactly what is meant by permissible levels of contact and are aware of all the necessary precautions to protect the participants.

Martial art competition involves the skilled utilisation of controlled techniques. It follows that this requires a high level of skill such as is not found in novices. No person should be allowed to compete until he has acquired the appropriate skill level.

In any system of competition which allows strong techniques, the participants should be evenly matched in terms of skill levels and physical characteristics. Some martial arts use weight and age divisions in individual events but not in team matches.

Safe training facilities

This is covered elsewhere in the book but suffice it to say here that the floor should be matted or sprung, and there should be no obstructions into the training area by pillars, steps, chairs, etc. When mats are used, they must be properly maintained. Class sizes must be monitored to prevent overcrowding.

Rehabilitation

Despite the precautions listed above, accidents will still occur and the coach should therefore be able to help the injured student back into training. However, this is not the same as treating an injury. Unless the coach is a qualified medical practitioner, or the injury is of an obviously minor nature, the coach must not attempt to treat it. In acute circumstances, first aid may be needed to deliver the injured party into medical care in as undeteriorated a condition as possible. A schedule of first aid practice is given on pages 152–66.

Rehabilitation is the gradual return of an injured part (or parts) to full functioning. It is speeded by the adoption of appropriate exercises and training methods.

The injured part may require a complete rest while the body is first mobilising its own healing processes. Sometimes it is sufficient merely to reduce training load on the affected part. Too much rest is a bad thing, leading to loss of flexibility in associated joints and wasting of the muscles. Localise rest to the area that needs it and continue to exercise the rest of the body as appropriate. Ice is very useful for reducing swelling and easing pain, but do not apply it direct to the skin over too long a period. Compression by means of a bandage further reduces swelling and gives valuable support. Elevation is yet another method for reducing swelling. The acronym for these procedures is 'RICE'.

Injuries such as cuts and lacerations need no special rehabilitation measures beyond covering them with a protective and hygienic dressing. While the laceration is healing, the injury site should not be subjected to further physical insult.

Joint damage is very common in martial art practice, but fortunately it benefits from the right kind of rehabilitative training. This achieves results by strengthening the muscles which work the joint. Isometrics are generally the best type of training for this purpose. Work should be gradually increased as the joint improves, but before subjecting it to high loadings there should be:

- an absence of pain, swelling and local feelings of heat
- a good range of active and passive movement at the joint
- normal strength in the muscles which act through the joint.

Strapping up the injured joint soon after beginning rehabilitation gives confidence, but as soon as possible the strapping must be removed. It is important that the joint is able to 'feel' naturally its angle at the earliest opportunity.

The ankle joint can be worked on a wobble-board (*see photograph 152*), the student steadying himself against a wall. As he becomes used to balancing on it, he can field and return an accurately thrown medicine ball. The muscles associated with knee and elbow joints can be strengthened first by isometrics and later by exercises which flex/extend the joint with its normal limits.

The wrist joint can be rehabilitated by isometrics and by exercises which move it through its full range of movement.

152. Working the ankle joints using a wobble-board. Lean against a wall until you can manage to balance unaided

Soft tissue injuries respond well to RICE. Injured muscles and tendons can be rehabilitated by moving them smoothly, and not using sudden explosive actions. Rehabilitation can begin when:

- the injured muscle can be gently stretched without pain
- the muscle generates its normal power output.

Bruises, haematomas and concussion can all be rehabilitated by allowing the injured tissues to recover without further physical insult to them.

Stress and anxiety

The body is not the only part of a martial artist to suffer injury and need rehabilitation. Stress and anxiety have a major effect upon performance, so the coach must know how to recognise and deal with them.

'Stress' and 'anxiety' cannot be easily defined in scientific terms, but we all know what is meant by them. The student begins to have doubts that he can cope with the demands he perceives he must face. This causes an emotional and physiological response which we interpret as anxiety.

A certain amount of anxiety before a competition or grading is no bad thing. In fact, it actually improves performance by making the student more alert and therefore more prepared to pick up significant cues upon which he can formulate a successful response. Blood is switched from the organs to the muscles in the 'vascular shunt', making the body ready for 'fight or flight'.

I recently saw what happened when a team failed to become aroused before the final of a tournament. Team 'A' fought its way through the earlier rounds with great panache, winning every match decisively. By comparison, team 'B' scraped through each round and didn't look in the same class as 'A'. During the interval, team 'A' just relaxed and some members even dozed off. By comparison, team 'B' were psyching themselves up and working away like fury. Came the final and – you've guessed it! – team 'B' won. By the time team 'A' grasped what was happening, it was too late.

If a small amount of anxiety is useful, an excess of it is definitely not! If the martial artist becomes too anxious, he suffers a dramatic collapse, and a significant lowering of anxiety is then necessary before performance can recover. As the anxiety level increases, the student:

- begins to worry about the outcome
- imagines the worst
- repeatedly uses the toilet
- has sweaty hands and a dry mouth
- feels sick and develops a racing pulse.

There are various other subtle effects, but I don't think we need dwell on them.

The coach must be alert to the more obvious symptoms because, if they are not controlled, feelings of panic set in and performance is ruined. Two things can help on the day. The first is letting the anxious student see his team-mates succeeding. It may be possible to alter team order so that he's moved from the more demanding first or last positions to third or fourth. If the first 2 team members do well, he is under less stress because, even if he fails, there are 2 more to come in behind him.

The team's reinforcement is a powerful antidote to anxiety. It follows, therefore, that teams should train together a great deal to build up strong feelings of inter-dependence.

The second and most used method to reduce anxiety is the coach's pep-talk. The student must be persuaded to re-evaluate both the magnitude of the perceived threat and his capability for dealing with it. This is sometimes difficult when the opponent towers over him and has just hospitalised the previous sparring partner! For the pep-talk to succeed, the coach must know the performer. Some students respond better when they are taken out of the immediate practice area to somewhere quieter. Others need to be in the training hall, but perhaps not watching what's actually happening. Speaking at the wrong time and in the wrong manner can increase anxiety rather than allay it.

In the longer term, anxiety is reduced most effectively by improving the student's confidence through target-setting. Another way is by meditation. At first this is difficult to achieve, and it is quite impossible to apply in the midst of a grading interval unless you are very experienced.

Meditation is taught in some martial art schools, though generally over too brief a period and without sufficient explanation to make it useful.

The way that works for me might work for you, too. Move as far away from distraction as possible and find somewhere comfortable to sit down. Keep your back straight and let your head incline forwards. Close your eyes and regulate your breathing so that it becomes slow and measured. Lightly press the tip of your tongue against the roof of your mouth and close your eyes.

At first your mind will be a riot of thoughts, but visualise that you are floating totally immersed in cold dark water, the current softly brushing against you. Try to feel the cold wetness of the water. If you try hard enough, your mind will gradually become quieter and, with a little practice, you can quiet your thoughts for 2 minutes or more at a time.

There is also a similar western-based anxiety reducing system known as 'Progressive Muscular Relaxation('PMR'). This recommends you to divide the muscle groups of your body into:

- shins and calves
- thighs and buttocks
- lower back and stomach
- chest, shoulders and arms
- neck and face.

Students lie back comfortably, or lounge in a chair with their eyes closed. They begin PMR by starting at the ankles and working upwards. First, they contract the target muscles, then relax them as fully as possible. Breathing is slow and regular and, with each expiration, a wave of relaxation deepens and spreads until the whole body is relaxed.

The drawback with both PMR and meditation is that they can lower the anxiety level until students become under-aroused. However, it does appear that if relaxation therapy is concluded a few minutes before performance is required, anxiety once more begins to climb – albeit more slowly than before.

It is often not a good idea to discuss the poor outcome of a grading or tournament immediately after failure. The coach should allow 1 or 2 days for the student to come to terms with it before giving an external appraisal. A positive feedback is then called for!

Nutrition

Nutrition is the name given to describe the way the body assimilates food. Food consists of carbohydrates, proteins, fats, vitamins, minerals, water and roughage. The relative amounts in which these are mixed together make up the diet.

The energy-producing value of foods is measured by a unit called the Calorie and it is estimated that the average person needs about 2,600 Calories per day. This rises according to the intensity of training to around 4,500 Calories.

When the body's energy requirements exceed that which is taken in, body reserves are used up and weight is lost. When Calorie intake exceeds energy requirements, body reserves are increased.

Digestion is the process by which the energy and nutrients in food are made available to the body. Food is broken down by a combination of mechanical and chemical action until it can be absorbed through the wall of the gut and into the bloodstream. The residue is excreted.

Carbohydrates are units of carbon, hydrogen and oxygen which exist in simple forms named **monosaccharides**, and more complex forms named **disaccharides** and **polysaccharides**. Monosaccharides are the basic units of energy production, so disaccharides and polysaccharides must first be broken down before they can be used. Carbohydrate is stored in the form of a polysaccharide called **glycogen**.

Taking in monosaccharides removes the need for the body first to break down more complex forms, so they provide a quick source of energy. Having said that, they are usually taken as refined carbohydrate which contains little else of nutritional value. By comparison, complex carbohydrates provide both the necessary energy and other nutrients as well.

A diet rich in carbohydrate provides energy for training. Without such a diet, martial artists simply cannot train as intensively as they might like. The body only stores sufficient carbohydrate to supply energy for about an hour or so of brisk training. After this, the carbohydrate reserve must be adequately replenished before hard training can resume. Replenishment should take the form of mixed simple and complex carbohydrate.

Proteins are very large compounds made from units named **amino acids**. These contain hydrogen, oxygen and nitrogen arranged in different ways. The process of digestion splits proteins into amino acids which are then recombined to make new body tissue. 21 different amino acids are used by the body in this way. Martial artists training intensively need protein to build new tissues. This is best taken in the form of white meat, fish, and/or a mixture of vegetable proteins.

Age range in years	Occupational category	Energy		Protein	Thiamin	Riboflavin	Nicotinic acid	Ascorbic acid	Vitamin A	Vitamin D	Calcium	Iron
		kcal	MJ	g	mg	mg	mg equiv	mg	μg retinol equiv[1]	μg chole-calci-ferol	mg	mg
Boys												
9 up to 12		2500	10.5	63	1.0	1.2	14	25	575	2.5	700	13
12 up to 15		2800	11.7	70	1.1	1.4	16	25	725	2.5	700	14
15 up to 18		3000	12.6	75	1.2	1.7	19	30	750	2.5	600	15
Girls												
9 up to 12		2300	9.6	58	0.9	1.2	13	25	575	2.5	700	13
12 up to 15		2300	9.6	58	0.9	1.4	16	25	725	2.5	700	14
15 up to 18		2300	9.6	58	0.9	1.4	16	30	750	2.5	600	15
Men												
18 up to 35	*Sedentary*	2700	11.3	68	1.1	1.7	18	30	750	2.5	500	10
	Moderately active	3000	12.6	75	1.2	1.7	18	30	750	2.5	500	10
	Very active	3600	15.1	90	1.4	1.7	18	30	750	2.5	500	10
35 up to 65	*Sedentary*	2600	10.9	65	1.0	1.7	18	30	750	2.5	500	10
	Moderately active	2900	12.1	73	1.2	1.7	18	30	750	2.5	500	10
	Very active	3600	15.1	90	1.4	1.7	18	30	750	2.5	500	10
65 up to 75	Assuming a	2350	9.8	59	0.9	1.7	18	30	750	2.5	500	10
75 and over	sedentary life	2100	8.8	55	0.8	1.7	18	30	750	2.5	500	10
Women												
18 up to 35	Most occupations	2200	9.2	55	0.9	1.3	15	30	750	2.5	500	12
	Very active	2500	10.5	63	1.0	1.3	15	30	750	2.5	500	12
55 up to 75	Assuming a	2050	8.6	51	0.8	1.3	15	30	750	2.5	500	10
75 and over	sedentary life	1900	8.0	48	0.7	1.3	15	30	750	2.5	500	10
Pregnancy 2nd and 3rd trimester		2400	10.0	60	1.0	1.6	18	60	750	10.0	1200	15
Lactation		2700	11.3	68	1.1	1.8	21	60	1200	10.0	1200	15

Table 2 Recommended intakes of nutrients

Department of Health and Social Security.

Recommended daily intakes of energy and nutrients for the UK.

	Vitamin	Sources	Involved in
A	Retinol or carotene	Liver, dairy produce, eggs, carrots, green leafy veg	Visual processes, connective tissue, skin
B_1	Thiamin	Meat, whole grains, legumes, nuts	Carbohydrate metabolism, CNS function
B_2	Riboflavin	Liver, diary produce, meat, cereal	Carbohydrate metabolism, vision, skin
B_6	Pyridoxin	Meat, fish, green leafy veg, whole grains, legumes	Protein metabolism, red blood cell formation, CNS function
B_{12}	Cyanocobalamin	Meat, fish, dairy produce; No vegetable sources	Red blood cell formation, CNS function
—	Niacin	Liver, meat, fish peanuts, cereal products	Carbohydrate and fat metabolism
—	Folic acid	Liver, legumes, green leafy veg	Regulates growth of cells, including red blood cells
C	Ascorbic acid	Green leafy veg, fruit, potatoes, white bread	Connective tissue, iron absorption/metabolism, healing/infection
D	Calciferols	Dairy produce, action of sunlight on skin	Calcium metabolism, bones and teeth
E	Tocopherols	Vegetable oils, liver, green leafy veg, dairy produce, whole grains	Protects vitamins A & C, and fatty acids, from destruction in body (anti-oxidant)
K	—	Green leafy veg and liver	Clotting of blood, fat digestion

Table 3

Fats are comprised of basic units named **triglycerides**. Like carbohydrates, they contain carbon, hydrogen and oxygen, though each unit contains relatively less oxygen. Digestion breaks fats down first into triglycerides and then into glycerol and fatty acids. The body uses fats both as a source of energy and to assist its normal functioning.

During exercise, the body uses fat from its reserves to help eke out the meagre supplies of stored carbohydrate. However, at maximum training intensity, only carbohydrate can provide energy fast enough, so it is quickly depleted whilst the fat is left relatively unused.

Overweight martial artists can reduce weight by reducing their intake of fats as part of a long-term change of eating habits. Crash diets deplete the body's car-bohydrate store and make prolonged intensive training impossible. Coaches should not, therefore, advise their students to lose too many kilos in order to make

Mineral	Sources	Involved in
Sodium	Salt, cheese, muscle/organ meat, fish/bacon	Neuromuscular transmission (nerve conduction) fluid and acid–base balance
Potassium	Meat, milk, veg, cereals, nuts	Neuromuscular transmission (nerve conduction) fluid and acid–base balance
Calcium	Milk, cheese, nuts, green veg, bread	Bone/tooth structure (nerve conduction), blood clotting
Magnesium	Green veg, meats, dairy produce, cereals	Neuromuscular transmission Bone formation, enzyme reactions – energy metabolism
Phosphorus	Grains and cereals, meat, milk, green veg	Bone/tooth formation, energy metabolism
Iron	Nuts/seeds, red muscle/organ meat, eggs, green veg	Haemoglobin/myoglobin formation
Zinc	Muscle meats, seafood, green veg	Enzyme synthesis
Copper	Shellfish, organ meats, nuts, legumes, cocoa/chocolate	Enzyme synthesis
Iodine	Seafood, eggs, dairy produce	Thyroid function
Fluoride	Seafood, water, tea	Tooth structure
Manganese	Nuts, dried fruit, cereals/grains, tea	Enzyme synthesis
Chromium	Meat and dairy produce, eggs	Glucose/insulin metabolism
Selenium	Seafood, organ and muscle meats and grains	Anti-oxidant (membranes) electron transfer

Table 4
Summary table of sources and functions of minerals

the weight. In such cases it is better they enter the next heavier weight division. Increasing weight is not so simple. This is best achieved through an increase in muscle mass developed through the correct form of training and supported by a high carbohydrate intake. Eating large amounts of protein-rich foods will only deplete the bank balance whilst producing great gusts of particularly nauseating flatulence as excess protein is broken down.

Vitamins are involved in the functioning of the body and a well-balanced diet provides an adequate supply. Vitamins B and C are water-soluble, whilst A, D, E and K are fat-soluble.

Many martial artists believe that supplementary vitamins are useful, but as yet there is no unbiased evidence to support this.

Minerals are essential for certain bodily functions. Potassium, for example, is necessary for the transmission of nerve impulses. Minerals are normally dissolved in the watery solution which bathes the living tissues. Water is the basic medium by which the body transports metabolites, and additionally it regulates the body's temperature through sweating.

The body's supply of water must be kept topped up by regular and moderate fluid intake. Salt tablets are unnecessary and should not be taken.

Questions

1 List ways of reducing the risk of injury during training.
2 Which medical condition precludes participation in martial art practice?
3 What precautions should be taken when coaching the following:
   a diabetics?
   b epileptics?
   c cardiac sufferers?
   d asthmatics?
4 What are the symptoms of fatigue?
5 What is required to ensure a safe competition?
6 What does 'rehabilitation' mean?
7 What does 'RICE' mean?
8 How would you rehabilitate an injured joint?
9 How would you rehabilitate a soft tissue injury?
10 What are the symptoms of escalating anxiety?
11 What can be done 'on the day' to alleviate anxiety?
12 Describe how you would meditate.
13 What is 'PMR'?
14 What are carbohydrates, proteins and fats?
15 How are they used in the body?
16 What are the functions of the following:
   a vitamins?
   b minerals?

PRACTICAL FIRST AID
FOR COACHES

Introduction

This is one of the most important chapters in the whole book, so don't read it until you have the time to do so thoroughly. If you allow enough time to understand the principles of first aid, you will be well on the way to making your training hall a safer place.

The good coach has a sound knowledge of first aid and the Martial Arts Commission recommends St. John's Ambulance Ordinary Level as the minimum qualification you should have.

What is first aid?

First aid is not about treating injuries. That is best left to a qualified person. First aid is about getting the victim of an accident to a place where he can be treated, in as good a condition as possible.

The basic principles of first aid are the following:

- don't panic!
- don't do anything you don't have to do
- if in doubt, do nothing but shout for help!

The first step in making a first aid response lies in recognising what you are dealing with. A correct diagnosis is essential to determine the right action to take.

As an example of a bad diagnosis, consider a situation in which the martial artist is found unconscious and with a badly gashed head. The priority here is to determine the reason for the unconsciousness and to deal with it. The gashed head is only a secondary consideration.

If it is impossible to decide how bad an injury is, then always pick the worst alternative, because then you won't do any harm and there is always the chance that you will be pleasantly surprised when you find it isn't as bad as you first thought it was.

To assist with your diagnosis, place the accident victim into one of two categories:

a   unconscious;
b   conscious.

The unconscious patient

Anyone who does not respond to, or is apparently unaware of, his surroundings can be regarded as unconscious. If he does not answer when you talk to him or he does not respond to a pinch, then consider the victim to be unconscious.

Actual unconsciousness may last only for a second or two, yet even so it is serious and shows that the brain has been damaged. Sometimes there is a sudden upsurge of vomit which can be inhaled and can block the airway.

Occasionally, a victim may remain on his feet, albeit unsteadily, and may respond to what you say. If you ask him his name he may respond, but it is obvious he is not really 'with it'. Ask him the date and where he is and, the chances are, the response will not be the same as if he were 'normal'. Treat such cases as though the victims are unconscious.

The next thing to discover is how the victim became unconscious in the first place. Whilst you apply first aid, ask his partner, or someone practising near by, what happened. Often this reveals useful facts to help your diagnosis.

There are 5 causes of unconsciousness and these are:

a   head injury
b   intracranial haemorrhage
c   cardiac arrest
d   insulin coma
e   hysteria.

Head injury

This happens as a result of a blow to the head caused by a fall, a throw, or an impact technique. Brain tissue is damaged and unconsciousness results.

Brain tissue is so delicate that it must be protected not only by the bones of the skull but also by membranes and a shock-absorbing fluid. A blow which violently moves the head causes brain tissue actually to move hard against the skull, causing death of many nerve cells. Even without this 'pile-up' against the bone, the delicate 'telephone wires' which connect the nerve cells are severed. Fortunately, the brain has a reserve of nerve cells which can, given rest and time, take over the functions of those which have died.

A strangulation hold will reduce or cut off the supply of blood to the brain, starving it of oxygen. When this happens, nerve cells cease to function and so unconsciousness and brain damage result.

Recovery after such injury is a slow process and patients must be withdrawn for a minimum period of at least 4 weeks from any activity which could lead to further damage. Brain tissue cannot be replaced; therefore, if a martial artist is repeatedly hit on the head over a long period of time, his intelligence will suffer.

Intracranial haemorrhage

In order for it to function, the brain must be nourished with oxygen and food supplied by a network of blood vessels which lie in and around the brain and its covering membranes. Bleeding between the membranes and skull produces pressure on the brain tissue, which leads to unconsciousness. This type of injury can be caused by a blow, or it can occur spontaneously through rupture of a blood vessel. The latter is called a 'stroke'.

If the haemorrhage is caused by a blow, then its particular symptoms may not appear for several hours after the blow has been struck. If the haemorrhage is caused by a stroke, the symptoms may appear very rapidly indeed.

Whichever is the cause, the symptoms are the same. The patient is unconscious and the complexion may be flushed. Breathing is often noisy and may appear forced. The pulse is slow. Sometimes there is a marked difference in size of the two pupils.

This last symptom occurs because an intracranial haemorrhage can affect only a part of the brain, so only a part of the body (usually one side) is affected. Someone suffering from this condition may look a little lop-sided when the muscles of one side of his face lose their tone and droop. The arm and leg on one side are often paralysed, too.

Note the following:

- a young person who has been knocked out, comes round and then becomes unconscious again, *has* got an intracranial haemorrhage
- a young person who suddenly becomes unconscious for no apparent reason *may* have an intracranial haemorrhage.

Intracranial haemorrhages require urgent treatment.

Cardiac arrest

Think of cardiac arrest as the heart ceasing to pump effectively, so that the brain becomes starved of oxygen and unconsciousness results. It takes about 15–30 seconds after the heart has stopped for a reduction in oxygen supply to the brain to take effect.

One cause of cardiac arrest in the martial arts is 'vagal inhibition'. The vagus nerve is responsible for slowing the rate at which the heart pumps blood. If suddenly and violently over-stimulated, it can cause cardiac arrest. The ways in which it can be over-stimulated are as follows:

a a blow – not necessarily hard – on the chest
b pressure on the neck (down which the vagus passes)
c sudden physical shock – such as being plunged into icy water
d sudden emotional shock – such as being badly frightened.

Vagal inhibition is most likely to happen when the martial artist is already in an excited condition. or under stress generated by a grading or a competition.

Cardiac arrest can also occur in martial artists who have recently suffered from a heavy virus infection. Certain virus infections seem to make heart muscle very irritable and a blow or shock leads to a cardiac arrest. Therefore, don't train hard during or after a virus infection. Allow about 2 weeks after the worst of the symptoms subside before training again.

The only other cause of cardiac arrest to concern the martial art coach tends to occur in the older student – though this is not to say it doesn't happen with younger people. In this case, blood supply to the heart muscle itself becomes blocked and the affected tissue dies.

The symptoms of cardiac arrest are the same in all cases – the victim loses consciousness and sometimes thrashes about. He may continue to breathe, but there will be no sign of a pulse. After a while, the victim's lips, ears and hands turn pale or bluish in colour. By this time it is probably too late to restart the heart.

Insulin coma

This only occurs in diabetic martial artists taking insulin. Diabetics need insulin to regulate the level of sugar in their blood and they estimate the amount to be taken each day. Sometimes a particularly heavy training session will use up more of their blood sugar than estimated for, so they become 'sugar starved'.

Onset of symptoms may be quite sudden and a victim may just collapse. At other times symptoms may appear gradually over a period of up to half an hour: as the blood sugar level drops, the patient behaves strangely, sweats profusely and/or may complain of feeling lightheaded or dozy. If you know that a particular person is diabetic, give him sugar and he will quickly recover.

Hysteria

Hysteria can mimic the effect of any of the previous causes of unconsciousness. Although it is mentally induced, the victim may be completely unaware of this. It is most often found in situations of great stress – such as during a competition or a grading. Never think that hysteria is to blame for the collapse of a student. Always consider the worst possible alternative and you will safeguard the victim.

The conscious victim

Dealing with conscious patients is much easier, because they can tell you where it hurts! When trying to find out what happened, be gentle, friendly and firm. Appear to be in complete control of the situation and look for obvious signs of injury.

Let's consider some options:

- no obvious signs of damage
- blood appearing where it shouldn't
- twisted or misshapen limbs, or pain associated with a bone
- lumps and bumps where they shouldn't be.

No obvious signs of damage

Consider the case in which the conscious patient suddenly becomes pale or grey in colour, is breathless, sweats profusely and complains of feeling cold. If this happens, summon help immediately, but do not allow the patient to lie down. There is a possibility that anyone experiencing these symptoms is having a heart attack. The following are classic symptoms of a heart attack and they may or may not occur together with those symptoms already described:

- a pain in the centre of the chest which often radiates down the arm(s)
- a feeling that there is a tight band around the chest.

Next consider a case in which the patient falls to the floor and then appears to rally slightly. He looks pale, complains of feeling cold, yet is sweating profusely. On examination, he is found to have a racing pulse.

To separate this condition from a heart attack, quietly ask whether the patient has received a very hard blow in the stomach area in the last hour or so. During the questioning, your assistants will have summoned help and you will be checking the pulse. If the victim has received a blow and does have a racing pulse, then you can assume that you are dealing with a case of 'surgical shock'.

This assumption is confirmed if the patient complains of tenderness, or pain over the lower ribs or at the tip of the respective shoulder. If the pain is just under the left ribs, you can assume that the spleen has been damaged; if it is under the right ribs, you can assume the liver has been affected.

A hard blow on the kidneys can cause internal bleeding, but this is not so great an emergency as a ruptured spleen or liver.

Hard blows can damage the internal organs to such an extent that they bleed into the trunk cavity. Unless halted, this loss of blood will rob the body of its means of carrying oxygen and food to vital organs such as the brain.

As internal bleeding continues, the heart rate speeds up to compensate. Once the level falls below a certain limit, the victim feels faint and may collapse onto the floor of the training hall.

Shock can occur whenever there is a blood loss of a pint or more – whether through internal bleeding or through external injury.

Though not strictly relevant to this section, you may be interested to hear what happened to the man who went on a sponsored breaking competition. On and on he went, until he finally collapsed with kidney failure! The damage the competition caused to his muscles released large quantities of a substance called **myoglobin** into the blood stream and it clogged his kidneys!

Sometimes the patient appears hard of hearing, or doesn't seem to know where he is, or what he is doing. In this case, despite appearances the patient may, in fact, be unconscious. It does not matter if he is still on his feet.

Blood appearing where it shouldn't

The correct place for the blood is in the body's arteries, veins and capillaries. Apart from the internal bleeding mentioned above, blood can be lost through a more obvious wound: damaged capillaries ooze blood; cut veins release a smooth flow of dark coloured blood; arteries spurt bright red blood.

Remember that if more than a pint of blood is lost, shock will set in.

Twisted or misshapen limbs

Where does the deformity occur? If it is at a joint, then you could be dealing with a dislocation. The affected joint will not operate and there will be an obvious shortening of one of its parts. For example, if a joint of the finger is dislocated, the further end of the finger may appear shortened.

If the arm sticks out at an odd angle, have a quick look to see whether the elbow or shoulder is dislocated. In both cases, the victim will effectively splint the injured limb by holding it in a comfortable position with the unaffected one. Don't attempt to move the joint about! Dislocations to the legs are very infrequent and need not be considered in this book.

A strain occurs when the ligaments which support a joint are torn, when a muscle is torn, or where there is a tear in the muscle/tendon or tendon/bone join. A sprain is a strained ligament. This type of injury is caused most often by incorrect warming up prior to a session. The affected area becomes extremely painful and swelling occurs.

Lumps and bumps

Fractures are breakages to the bone, ranging from a simple crack to a smashed bone which projects through the skin. Any fracture associated with broken skin is called a 'compound fracture'. These are more serious than simple breaks.

The fracture is found either at the site of an impact or twist, or some distance from it. For example, a common type of fracture occurs when someone falls and puts out a straight arm to protect himself. This commonly results in a fracture – not at the wrist – but higher up the arm. Regardless of where it is, the site of the breakage will be, at the very least, painful to touch.

Fractured ribs make breathing difficult, but they don't threaten life. If the broken rib has pierced a lung, breathing will be seriously affected and only the uninjured side of the chest will be seen to move. Sometimes it is possible to feel a crackling sensation under the skin at the site of the injury, as air leaks through the tissues. A broken neck is one of the most serious forms of fracture. Moving the head in relation to the body can break the spinal cord and paralyse the victim for life. Unfortunately, a broken neck cannot be readily seen and the only practical diagnosis comes from the conscious patient. Broken necks are not only caused by a direct strike to the neck, but they can also be caused by a whiplash injury.

Bone is well supplied with blood through an overlying membrane. A heavy blow over an uncushioned bone can cause loss of blood into the immediate area of the injury. In bad cases, an actual lump called a **haematoma** indicates where blood is collecting.

A hernia is caused by a sudden strain tearing the muscles of the stomach wall. It can happen to fit young people as well as to older martial artists and is seen as a lump or swelling at the site of the injury. It occurs in the groin or indeed anywhere over the surface of the abdomen.

The basic procedures

The unconscious patient

The basic procedures you must learn to apply to the unconscious patient are:

- detecting a pulse
- cardiac massage
- checking for breathing
- artificial respiration
- moving the patient.

These have not been listed in any specific order of importance. Several of your regular club members must learn these procedures, because there may come a time when you are required to practise two simultaneously and you will obviously need help.

Detecting a pulse
Don't bother with groping around the wrist – turn your attention to the front of the neck. Look for the windpipe which runs down the centre of the neck, and slide the tips of your fingers down the side of it until they encounter muscle. When you reach the muscle, probe in gently with your fingers to locate the carotid artery – there's one on each side of the neck, so you can't miss it (*see photograph 153 on page 161*). Don't press too hard!

Cardiac massage
Turn the patient onto his back on a firm surface, such as the floor. Open the patient's mouth and have a good look to check it is clear of false teeth, plates or gumshields that may be caught at the back of the throat. If in doubt, feel around the back of the throat with your fingers and, if you find any foreign object, clear

Unconscious patient

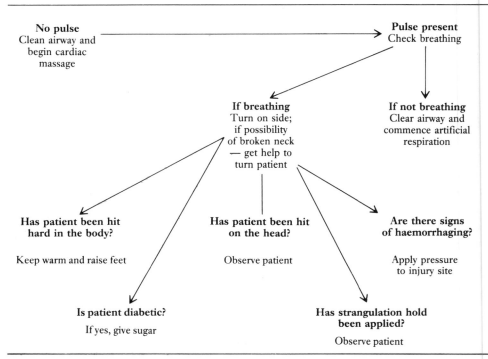

Figure 1 Emergency procedures for the unconscious patient

it. If vomit is present, clean it out with your fingers, some tissue or a piece of tunic. Kneel astride the patient's waist and face his head. If you are alone and will also have to perform artificial respiration, then kneel at the patient's side. Run your fingers down the centre line of his chest until you find the end of the breast-bone, then move up 2 inches or so. Make a fist with one hand and then wrap the other hand round it so that the bases of the two palms are together and the wrapping fingers overlay the closed fingers of the fist.

Raise up off your haunches and, resting your linked hands on the lower third of the breast-bone, straighten your elbows and use full body weight to compress it (*see photograph 154*). Apply weight sharply, driving the breast-bone inwards by about one and a half inches. If you have done this correctly, your assistant will feel a corresponding pulse at the carotid.

Repeat this 60 times a minute until either the pulse picks up of its own accord or until a doctor tells you the patient is dead. Unless effective cardiac massage is started within 2 minutes of the arrest, it will probably be impossible to restart the heart.

If you are unaided, apply 4 sharp pressures, then ventilate the patient's lungs once. Repeat this cycle as necessary.

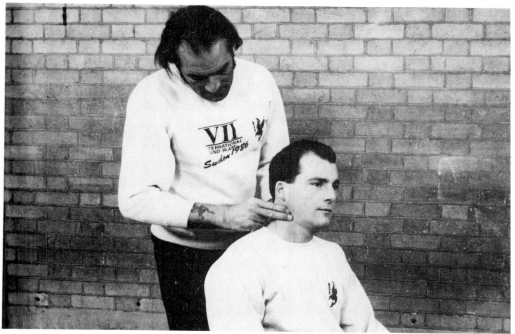

153. Locating the carotid artery on the side of the neck

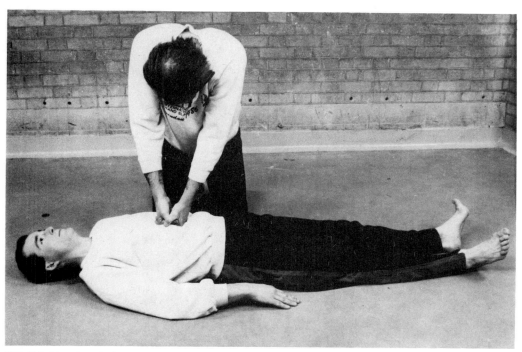

154. Linking hands before applying weight onto the breast-bone

Do not practise cardiac massage on a friend or student, because if done properly it can break ribs!

Checking for breathing

Perform this check when the patient is still, because handling can compress the chest and make you think that he is breathing whereas, in fact, he is not.

Put your ear next to the patient's mouth and nostrils. Listen for breaths and feel for the wash of warm air over your ear which signals that the patient is breathing.

Artificial respiration

First, clear the airway as previously described. This by itself may cause breathing to restart. If breathing does not restart, then apply artificial respiration.

Tilt the patient's head backwards and, with the other hand, push the jaw forwards using the thumb and index finger (*see photograph 155*). If this is not done, the tongue can fall back and block the airway. Pinch the patient's nostrils closed; then take a good breath and apply your mouth firmly to the patient's, making sure there is a good seal. Breathe out firmly, so the patient's chest rises; then, withdraw your mouth and allow the patient to breathe out naturally. Repeat this procedure 10–15 times a minute until the patient starts breathing naturally.

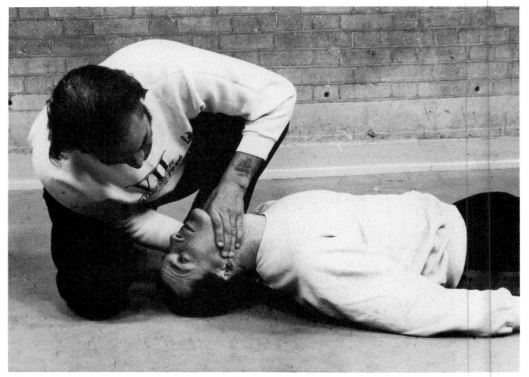

155. Tilt the head back and the jaw forwards in preparation for artificial respiration

Moving the patient

If you have any grounds at all for believing that the unconscious patient may have a broken neck, then disturb him as little as possible. Check the patient is breathing and has a pulse. Prevent him from inhaling vomit by turning him. Whilst doing this, *do not* allow his head to fall towards his chest.

The conscious patient

Basic procedures to be applied to the conscious patient are:

- halting a haemorrhage
- dealing with a dislocation
- coping with a fracture
- dealing with strains and sprains
- coping with hernias.

Halting a haemorrhage

Loss of blood to an internal cavity leads to surgical shock. Lay the patient out flat and keep him warm. If the patient still feels faint, lift his legs and support them with a rolled coat. Assure the patient that help is on its way. Do not give him anything to drink.

Loss of blood to the outside is treated by applying pressure to the part that is bleeding. If you have a handkerchief, a tissue wad or a towel, so much the better. Clamp it firmly over the bleeding with your fingers and hold it there. If you don't have a pad, press with your fingers.

If the arm is badly gashed, make the patient do a 'Seig heil' salute and hold the arm up high. This, plus a pad applied as described, will rapidly stop the flow. You can, of course, do the same to a leg, but it is rather undignified for the poor patient who is, in any case, unlikely to expire provided you clamp the pad on tightly.

Do not apply tourniquets!

In the case of a cut throat, prompt action is called for to save life. Put a pad on the area, applying pressure above and below the site of the cut.

If there is a haematoma, suspect bony injury and send the patient to his doctor. Applying ice will ease the condition.

Dealing with dislocations

Do not attempt to reduce these yourself. Take the injured party quickly to hospital – delay can make reduction of a dislocation more difficult. Allow the patient to hold the dislocated limb in a comfortable position.

Coping with fractures

Do not attempt to deal with these yourself. If coping with a fracture of the arm, let the patient brace that limb in a comfortable position and take him directly to the hospital. If a leg is broken, call an ambulance and do not move the patient.

Keep the patient warm and do not give him anything to eat or drink. If the fracture is compound, cover the laceration with a clean dressing.

It should not be necessary to move a patient with a broken leg and attempts to do so will only cause severe distress. Nevertheless, if it is essential, then bind the injured leg to the uninjured one and gently move the patient with the aid of assistants.

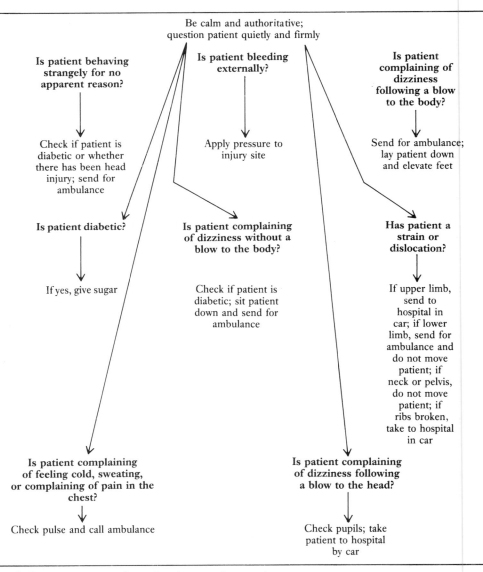

Conscious patient

Figure 2 Emergency procedures for the conscious patient

Patients with fractured ribs may be taken to hospital. Wrap them up warmly, but do not apply pressure over the injured part.

An awkward fall can cause a fracture of the pelvis, but this is not as bad as it sounds. Much worse is when the pelvis is actually crushed, but thankfully this occurrence has not yet been reported in martial art practice. The patient with a fractured pelvis will complain of pain in his back or legs. He should not be moved and an ambulance should be sent for.

Dealing with strains and sprains
First aid for sprains and strains is ice application. An ice-bag applied to the site will greatly relieve pain and suffering. If you don't have an ice-bag, use a packet of frozen peas or even a cold damp towel.

Coping with hernias
You cannot deal with these yourself. Send the patient to his doctor. The condition needs no immediate treatment and there is no cause for panic.

Common sense

Check out the following points.

1 Ensure that at least two first aiders are present at each training session.
2 Identify the exits to the premises and make sure that you and your students know the whereabouts of a working public telephone.
3 Know where to find your local hospital with an Accident or Casualty Unit.
4 Provide at least one doctor for all tournaments or major courses.
5 Keep a first-aid kit at your premises and make sure that its whereabouts and the whereabouts of the key to it are known to students. The most basic kit must contain:

- paper tissues (a roll of lavatory paper will do)
- a pair of stout scissors (lightweight snips are best)
- a triangular bandage and a packet of safety pins
- crêpe or foam bandage
- an eye patch
- a small bottle of disinfectant
- a bottle of painkillers, such as asprin or paracetamol.

6 Keep a warm blanket with your first-aid kit.
7 Do not overcrowd the training hall.
8 Do not mis-match partners. Pair according to weight and reach (the distance between the middle fingertips of the widely extended arms).
9 Do not train on a solid floor, because falls on it can and have caused serious injury.

10 If you use mats, be sure that they are firmly attached to each other. Site the training area away from all hazards, such as radiators and chairs. Keep the floor space uncluttered.

Questions

1 What are the 5 causes of unconsciousness?
2 How can you tell if someone is unconscious?
3 Can damaged brain tissue ever regenerate?
4 What is an 'intracranial haemorrhage'?
5 What is a 'stroke'?
6 What are the causes of heart attacks?
7 What is 'vagal inhibition'?
8 What precautions should be taken concerning students with virus infections, and why are these needed?
9 Describe the symptoms of a heart attack.
10 How is a heart attack caused?
11 What is an insulin coma?
12 How may it be treated?
13 What is hysteria?
14 What signs of obvious injury do you look for?
15 How is surgical shock caused?
16 Which parts of the body can become dislocated?
17 What does a classic dislocation look like?
18 What is a strain?
19 What is a fracture?
20 What is a hernia?
21 Where is the carotid pulse found?
22 Describe how to administer cardiac massage.
23 How should you check that the patient is breathing?
24 Describe how to administer artificial respiration.
25 How should you deal with surgical shock?
26 How should you stop a haemorrhage?
27 How should you deal with fractures?
28 How should you deal with a hernia sufferer?
29 List 10 points of common sense concerned with safety.

COACHING AND THE LAW

Introduction

In this chapter I am going to set out how the law affects you, the martial art coach. During my 10 years as General Secretary of the Martial Arts Commission I gained a great deal of practical experience in this aspect of coaching. I often attended court as an 'expert witness' and regularly corresponded with solicitors acting on both sides of a dispute. I even worked with the Home Office on the thorny (and still unresolved) problem of martial arts weapons. All this made me aware how the law can affect every aspect of martial art practice.

This chapter summarises my experiences in what amounts to a very complicated field. However, as new cases crop up with increasing frequency, it is up to you, the coach, to regard this chapter only as a starting point.

I have tried to steer away from legal jargon, but let me just explain two terms which crop up from time to time. The first is 'plaintiff'. In practical terms, the plaintiff is the injured party in an action, whilst the second, the 'defendant', is the party being sued/prosecuted.

The club premises

A martial art instructor decided to open a new club in a little town just outside London. The only facilities available were a church hall, but this had a concrete floor covered with thin composition tiles. Nevertheless, the instructor took out a hiring and began his club there. All went well until one evening when he finished off training with a spot of free-sparring. Two students were going at each other with great gusto, until one fell and banged his head against the floor. The result was permanent brain damage.

The brain-damaged chap happened to be a trainee chef with brilliant prospects. Now he has no prospects and the quality of his life has been seriously reduced. The family is taking the instructor to court on the grounds that he was negligent in allowing martial art practice in unsuitable premises. It is also suing the hirers of the church hall. The case against the defendants is legally-aided and has a very good chance of success.

Then there's the case of another club in the Midlands which took the trouble to buy and maintain a good mat. Unfortunately, the training area was a little cramped, so there was no adequate run-off area around the edge of the mat. Consequently, one chap was thrown clean through a glass door and all but severed his right hand. The hand has been saved, but its function is badly impaired. The injured party is suing the club instructor for negligence.

There is also the case of a northern club which operates in first floor facilities. One night a bulb in the upper landing failed and a young girl, on her way out after training, tripped and fell down the stairs. She is suing the club instructor.

These three examples serve to show that any person operating a martial art club is liable in law to make all reasonable efforts to ensure that the facilities are suitable for the purpose, and that they are adequately maintained in a safe condition.

What if you hire premises? Begin by reading the terms under which you hire them. A sports centre, for example, has some responsibility for the activities it allows to take place within its walls. Nevertheless, do still keep an eye on things and report any deficiencies to the duty manager.

Each martial art governing body sets its own requirements with regard to training safety and it is your responsibility as coach to make sure you know what these are. The following general points apply across the board:

- the training hall must be large enough to allow students present to train without undue risk of collision with one another. If an injury occurs because you allowed the training area to become overcrowded, then you may be held responsible. The best alternative is to divide up your classes. The next best thing is to stagger training to that one half of the class looks on whilst the other trains; then the students change around.

- the training hall must be adequately heated and ventilated. Emergency exits must be clearly marked and kept unobstructed. An emergency evacuation procedure must be made known to all class members.

- access/exit to the training hall must be safe. Obviously you aren't responsible for the state of the roads or public transport, but once a student comes into the area you have hired, you assume responsibility for him. Check with the owners of the property to see who is responsible for maintaining the entry and exit ways.

- no unguarded glass doors or windows should be within a minimum of 3 metres of the training area. Glass within this distance should be adequately covered by mesh, or replaced with safety glass of an approved standard.

- light fittings must be an adequate height above the training surface to allow the proper execution of technique. In one training hall, the fittings were high enough for normal training but not for weapons practice. An overhead fluorescent tube was shattered, with the result that several students got badly cut feet. The level of illumination must be adequate for an activity which relies upon controlled techniques. The eye sees detail only in conditions of bright illumination.

- all supporting pillars and central heating radiators within 3 metres of the training area must be adequately padded. There is a case on record where a man was knocked off balance and suffered a compound fracture of his right forearm when it struck the edge of a pillar. Mirrors, too, must be away from the training area because they are difficult to sight on. One student was practising his reverse punch to a mirror, but he misjudged the distance and hit it. The glass shattered and he needed microsurgery to restore the use of his fingers. Wallbars are also potentially dangerous.

■ the coach must see that the floor is kept clear, level and uncluttered to permit unhindered movement both on and around the training surface. Don't let bags obstruct the area.

■ onlookers and non-participants must sit at least 3 metres away and should not obstruct free movement around the edges of the area. Bear this in mind when you organise a championship. Don't crowd spectators around the mat and do appoint stewards to keep the edges of the area clear. This is essential.

■ the training surface must be kept clean and free from splinters. Sweep it before the day's training session. The surface must be non-slip, even after prolonged training. Did you see the television programme which showed martial artists sliding and slipping about all over the place? As luck would have it, no injuries occurred but, had they done so, the club instructor could have been one of those sued for allowing practice to continue despite obviously dangerous conditions.

■ if mats are used, then secure them properly together so they can't move apart. The coach must regularly inspect them during the training session. I've lost count of the number of competitions I've seen where gaps opened between mats. A world class female martial artist suffered a broken ankle when it twisted between separated mats. Had she taken the matter further, she could have sued both the referee and the tournament organisers. I am not convinced that mats are necessary for general training purposes in all martial arts, but nevertheless the floor must have some degree of 'give' to it.

■ a safe place should be provided for students to leave their valuables. Where this is not provided, students must be informed and allowed to bring their valuables into the training room. I know of one case where a new leather coat was stolen from the changing room. No warning notices were displayed, so the club coach was held to be responsible by the plaintiff.

■ location of the nearest open hospital casualty unit must be known. The club must provide access to a fully stocked first aid kit before, during and after training.

The coach who observes these recommendations will be unlikely to fall foul of the law with respect to his training premises.

Some coaches feel these requirements are too strict, but this may not be the opinion of the judge hearing a negligence case.

Club equipment

An international federation decided to enforce usage of a particular type of fist protector at its competition, ostensibly because someone in that federation thought it was safe. In practice it turned out to be dangerous. When a punch was thrown, the padding moved back from the knuckles it was supposed to cushion and exposed a seam-edge capable of inflicting serious cuts.

A young male competitor was hit in the eye with one of these and was injured. Both he and his national federation might well have separately sued the international federation. The national federation had made an investment of several thousand pounds in that competitor's training and this was all lost through insistence on using dangerous equipment.

In view of this, should you recommend safe equipment? Is it not part of the coach's duty to give guidance to students in this respect? Consider the following.

A martial art contestant decided to adhere to the rules of competition and to wear a groin guard. In the absence of guidance from his coach, he chose one that slips inside a jockstrap. During the bout, he threw a number of high kicks and the box became displaced. An incoming low kick from the opponent caught the box square-on and the testicle trapped outside was badly damaged by the edge of the box.

Did the coach fail in his responsibility in this respect? Should he not have explained that such protectors are unsuitable for martial art competition? That particular incident didn't go to court, but the next one may well do so.

The message is clear. Ensure that your association recommends safe equipment, and do not promote alternatives. Keep an eye on its performance and alert your association to any defects. Where your association does not make a specific recommendation, contact the Martial Arts Commission and they will obtain advice for you.

However, even the best advice is not a 100% guarantee that litigation cannot arise. Consider the case of the association that required, as part of its grading syllabus, a demonstration of the force generated by techniques. It provided a breaking horse made exactly to international governing body specifications. The required number of wooden boards were slotted in and the trainee was invited to break them with a kick. He didn't succeed in breaking the boards, but he did manage to break his foot.

The matter is proceeding to court and the plaintiff contends that the design of the breaking horse is inherently unsafe, because there is an insufficient margin for user-safety built into it. What happens is that when the foot misses the board — as it can all too easily do with spinning kicks — the foot connects with the sharp-edged and substantial frame!

The coach's competence to teach

You may have a black belt, but how do you know you are competent and safe to teach others? Does your association only train students in terms of skill to black belt level and then turn them loose on unsuspecting students? If the answer to this is 'yes', then your association is being negligent.

It is not for the black belt to say he is competent to coach, any more than he can assess his own skill level and give himself an advancement in grade.

What happens then, when he does something silly, a student is injured and he faces court proceedings as a result? First of all, if he has been negligent – that is to say, if he has failed in his responsibilities – he will be involved in the action. Secondly, because his association allowed him to teach, then by implication it has accepted his coaching ability. So, it also gets brought into the affair.

It may happen, too, that the governing body to which his association belongs is taken to court as well – even though it may never have seen that instructor before. At first consideration this might seem unfair but it is justified in this way:

■ in accepting his association into membership, the governing body has satisfied itself that it is a fit and proper organisation, capable of operating established standards. The governing body is therefore held to be responsible for ensuring that all its federal members continue to conduct themselves properly, even after they are taken into membership. If it fails to do this, then it can be regarded as negligent.

Whole chains of defendants are not uncommon, because solicitors will want to get as much damages as possible for their client and the club instructor alone may not have sufficient resources.

Bear this in mind if you are a club instructor with assistant instructors. Do the assistants have a formal qualification given by your association to assist you? If not, then you are taking risks. Even if they are qualified, how far can they be entrusted with running the class?

What happens if you can't make training one night and you ask an assistant to take the class for you? If all goes well, nothing happens, but if there is an injury, then you may be held liable because you entrusted the class to an assistant coach, i.e. a person who only **assists** the coach.

The assistant coach works always under your supervision and never alone. This is not, of course, to say that you cannot pop out to the toilet and leave the class in his care for a couple of minutes; but you may not leave the class to have a smoke or to make a non-emergency telephone call.

The habit of entrusting beginners to the assistant coach is a bad one, because the latter has neither the skill nor the coaching ability to teach properly and to correct beginners. In consequence, they quickly acquire bad habits which may be difficult to eradicate later. More importantly, beginners are a high injury risk group and require expert supervision for their safety.

New students joining the club

All kinds of people apply to join martial art clubs – unhealthy as well as healthy, anti-social as well as social. It therefore makes good sense to check all applications before accepting them.

Are students capable of enduring the type of training you do in your club? There's one way to find out, of course – pitchfork them into the middle and let them discover for themselves! But what happens if one student has a heart condition and falls ill during training? It will be no good saying 'I didn't know he had a bad heart' if you made no effort to find out before accepting his application.

Use a proper application form like the one set out on page 188. Ask new students to declare such health conditions as heart trouble, haemophilia, diabetes, epilepsy, asthma, etc. If a form comes back declaring a listed condition, send the student to his doctor for medical clearance before accepting him. If a student makes a false declaration, it is hardly your responsibility thereafter.

It is a good idea to allow prospective students to watch training, so they can judge for themselves whether they can manage it. Recommend students over the age of 40 to take a medical examination before they begin training.

Having dealt with health considerations, what about students who have convictions for crimes of violence? Is it a good idea to teach martial art to habitual rapists or child molesters? How do *you* ensure that people you train are responsible enough to receive the knowledge you are imparting to them? You may not be responsible for any subsequent crimes they may commit, but you may well achieve undesirable publicity.

'Have you ever been convicted of a crime of violence?' is the question posed by the recommended application form. If the applicant declares a 'no' response, then short of hiring a team of private investigators, you cannot take the matter further. If the applicant has lied, you have the signed application form as justification for teaching him.

What do you do if the applicant gives a 'yes' response? Obviously the first thing is to interview him to discover the facts. Did it happen a long time ago, with no recurrence since? Were there mitigating circumstances? These are all factors to consider. Some coaches claim that practising a martial art can rehabilitate offenders. This may be so, but do not set yourself up as an amateur psychiatrist.

There has been a lot of discussion about the value, or otherwise, of disclaimers which say things to the effect that 'The club disclaims any liability for injuries, mutilations, castrations, disembowelments and deaths arising out of any acts, errors or omissions by its coaching staff or their servants'. The fact is: no one can sign away his rights in law, so such a disclaimer is worthless.

What you can do, however, is to include a statement to the effect that 'Having seen the practice of martial art as carried on in the club, and having had explained to me that this practice may result in injury, I have voluntarily agreed nevertheless to apply for membership to the said club'. A disclaimer of this type may possibly weaken the plaintiff's assertion that he didn't realise what practice involved when he joined.

No sensible coach allows students onto the training area until they have applied and paid for a Martial Arts Commission licence. Allow no free first lessons and do not put off registering all students (juniors and seniors) until the first grading. Bear in mind that medical statistics prove that many injuries occur early on in training. It is therefore commonsense to provide students with an insurance policy which not only covers them against personal accident, but which more importantly indemnifies them against the risk of causing injury to other students.

The M.A.C. personal accident policy operates from the time the student completes the application form and passes it to the coach for validation. It does not matter whether you then send completed forms to the registrar, or the student sends them direct. I would advise the former, because then you are sure the form has been properly completed and sent off promptly. This is important, since the registrar of your association only has a limited time to process the return; if, for any reason there is a delay, insurance cover will lapse.

Do make your licence returns at least once a week. Who do you think would be held responsible if through your delay an injured student was denied insurance compensation?

The club coach must also be continuously covered against negligence. You may say (as indeed many have) that you do not teach for money, gifts, services, expenses, or for any other kind of material reward, so why should you take out this indemnity? The reasons are quite straightforward:

- the member–to–member cover in your basic licence will certainly cover you if you injure someone you are teaching, but it will not indemnify you if the person you told to fight another proved negligent
- the member–to–member cover does not offer high enough benefits for teaching purposes; did you know that one coach (not of martial art, I hasten to add) was sued for having insufficient professional indemnity?

Dangerous practices

Every student has a right to be taught authorised techniques in a proper and safe manner. I once had to appear for the plaintiff in an action against a Metropolitan Police self-defence instructor, because during introductory self-defence training the police coach clapped his cupped hand over the plaintiff's ear, rupturing his eardrum. This technique was not, it turned out, an approved police technique, so the instructor was successfully sued. Had the technique been part of the official syllabus, then an action against the Metropolitan Police would have proceeded. The fact is that no one goes to a training session expecting to be injured. The coach must be capable of organising and supervising a training session, competition or event in such a way that it is reasonably safe. Teach only those techniques approved by your association and don't be tempted to experiment on students. If the approved techniques are subsequently proven to be dangerous, then some of the burden of responsibility must transfer to your chief instructor.

Ensure you teach techniques commensurate with the ability of the students. Don't be tempted to show advanced techniques to novices, because injury may occur through lack of control or skill. You may recall that in Chapter 1 I mentioned the dangers of introducing free-sparring too early on.

Be careful when matching students – especially during free-sparring. Match for age and weight, and never pit a child, however skilled, against an adult unless you know the latter is sensible, skilful and controlled. Be careful, too, when matching men against women. Do not spar when you should be supervising the class. Many of us like to join in but, if we do, how can we supervise the other bouts?

Are procedures for warming up the class set down in your association? Do you have specified exercises which are known to be effective and safe? Treat exercises in the same way that you treat techniques and make certain they are properly taught and supervised.

Even well recommended exercises may give you cause for concern. Consider the bodyweight exercise for developing the abdominals which has Fred kneeling on all fours whilst Jim sits on his shoulders, feet linked below Fred's chest. Jim is supposed to lean backwards, but if he is too heavy, or Fred is either tired or his upper body musculature is weak, then he is likely to suddenly collapse forwards as Jim leans backwards (*see photograph 156*).

There is no substitute for observation, evaluation and common sense.

Violence, training method and competition rules

I well recall kneeling in class lines waiting to be beaten up by the chief instructor! He used to strap a little foam pad to his instep – not I suspect to save us pain, but rather to protect some ancient injury. Then he would simply batter us unmercifully!

On one occasion a man from a different style visited us. He asked the chief instructor to free-spar, but he was directed instead to the assistant chief instructor. Within five seconds, the visitor was unconscious with a badly fractured jaw that hospitalised him for weeks afterwards. By dint of grovelling apology, the secretary of our association only just succeeded in staving off a very expensive litigation and criminal proceedings.

A similar case actually went to court and the defendant called a senior instructor from his association as expert witness. Said witness claimed it was custom and practice to beat up students! The judge accepted this submission, but went on to point out that what takes place in a martial art association is not exempt from the rule of law simply because students apparently consent to it.

The law expects the highly competent person to exercise greater skill in controlling

156. This is a recommended exercise, but I believe it is dangerous. What do you think?

techniques than the novice. So, not only must coaches be careful in their physical interraction with students, but they must also ensure that the students do not physically abuse each other! Supposing you have a student in your club who is always injuring his partners. Do you allow him to continue until one day he lands in court, with you joined to the action?

Competitive martial arts raise further issues. Consider those which permit only controlled contact. In a case still to be heard, two members of a squad were competing for a place in the team under the supervision of the national coach. One caught the other in the eye with his big toe, causing permanent 60% loss of vision in that eye.

If this proceeds to court, the issues to be considered will be:

a   was the bout being conducted in accordance with properly devised rules?
b   are those rules in accordance with the law of the land?
c   was the bout in question being supervised by a properly qualified person with a knowledge of the rules?
d   did the person causing the injury act in a malicious manner?

Assume for discussion purposes that reasonable rules were being applied by a qualified referee. The plaintiff will have to show that the defendant intended deliberately to contravene the rules. This may prove difficult.

The coach must be aware that it is not legal to organise any event under rules which by their very content create a likelihood of serious injury or death.

Several martial art associations organise competitions, yet they do not train referees. They are obviously unaware that competitors have a right to expect supervision by a properly qualified referee who knows and can enforce the rules of safety.

The referee must strictly apply the rules, since, poor though they may be, they are his only safeguard. All coaches who prepare competitors for events should attend refereeing courses to become fully aware of the rules.

Many coaches organise inter-club courses and championships, but are they aware of the responsibilities this entails? They know the standards, health and behaviour of their own students, but what of the visitors? The possibilities for litigation are many, so the organising coach must obtain appropriate insurance cover. Even so, this cover may not allow carte-blanche for the coach to flout every safety rule in the book!

The sensible coach must:

- take out an insurance idemnity for the event, with benefits large enough to cover accepted levels of liability
- select a venue suitable for the purpose
- screen all participants for health risks by means of an application form
- check that all participants have a current Martial Arts Commission licence on the day of the competition
- provide a suitably surfaced, safe competition area of specified size
- provide a minimum level of qualified first aid or medical cover throughout the event
- provide sufficient properly qualified officials

Children and martial arts

Children flock to martial art classes in their thousands and the good coach must consider the following two points:

a there is a heavy responsibility upon the coach to ensure that children are returned to their families after training in the same condition as that in which they came

b children cannot be expected to show as much restraint as adults when it comes to using the martial art techniques they have learned against other children.

In several instances where a child has taken a few knocks in training, irate parents have threatened legal action. Avoid this by making sure parents visit the club before the child is allowed to join. Invite them to watch a session. Never allow a person below the age of 18 years to join without parental permission. Note that the recommended application form carries a consent form.

Girls and boys in their mid-teens may not appreciate having to bring their mums and dads along, so allow them to take the consent forms home for signature. Nevertheless, do enclose a note with the application form, inviting parents to try to attend if at all possible.

Here's something you may not have thought about. Does your responsibility end when the session finishes? Who is responsible when the session runs over time and the child misses the bus and has to walk back home? Not all parents own cars! Children require constant supervision. A case went to court because a child was injured when she fell heavily whilst playing in the training area. The coach hadn't even arrived then! Another case concerned a young chap who damaged his hand breaking wood in a demonstration arranged by his coach.

Many training regimes and exercises cannot safely be imposed on children. Be especially careful when allowing them to spar and always be mindful of the non-martial art case where a teacher tackled and injured a 15-year-old boy. He was successfully sued because, although the tackle was within the rules, the teacher should have taken his own greater power and weight into account.

Some associations permit boys to fight girls, and young competitors are not adequately graded according to height/reach, weight and experience. One association even allows children to use full contact kicks to the head! All these are accidents waiting to happen.

Let's now look at the second point. The coach cannot expect to evade responsibility if the kick he has taught a child is used to inflict injury in the playground. Children must not be taught techniques which can be easily adapted for use in fighting. There is plenty of scope within a martial art syllabus to maintain interest without equipping children to damage each other. If an association welcomes young members, then it must be able to offer something which is safe not only for them but also for their non-practising playmates.

Martial arts and self defence

The courts recognise no martial art novices! Anyone with a passing knowledge of martial art is regarded as an 'expert'. This leads to unbalanced judgements.

Part of the attraction of martial arts lies in the mystique surrounding them. Exaggerated claims of effectiveness have led to the courts assuming that every martial artist is potentially more dangerous than every other member of the public. Consider the following case.

A young black belt took his girlfriend to a disco where she was pestered by two young men. The manager threw the men out, so they waited outside and waylaid the black belt as he left. He broke one chap's jaw and fractured the other's ribs. They reported him to the police and he was subsequently convicted of inflicting actual bodily harm.

His two assailants were members of a local amateur boxing club, but this didn't count because the court expected him to exercise a greater measure of restraint than he did.

Coaches must bear in mind that:

a   courts have the benefit of 20/20 hindsight. They know how the confrontation came out. The defence must try to bring out the fear, uncertainty and spontaneity of the moment.

b   the court will assume that every martial artist has the ability to inflict physical damage out of all proportion to their stature and actual ability. Defence must try to give a truer picture of their status, perhaps by reference to a senior coach from the same association.

c   the court will expect all martial artists to be more likely to inflict injury upon their assailant(s) than untrained persons. Defence must again try to put effectiveness in true perspective.

The coach must make all students aware of the philosophy of traditional martial art – which is that the victor is the one who avoid confrontation. When violence is unavoidable, students must respond with only enough force to ensure their own safety. Students may actually strike first to gain tactical advantage, but only when threatened with imminent and obvious violence.

Martial arts and weapons training

Though there is relatively little evidence to support it, the press and media are convinced that martial art weapons constitute a danger to the public. Whether as the cause or effect of this publicity, the police are taking a greater interest in martial art weapons, and prosecutions increase in number each year.

The law dealing with weapons other than flick-knives and firearms is so vague as to allow the police to arrest anyone found in possession of anything which could be used as a weapon. To get a conviction, they must prove that the defendant intended to use the item as a weapon.

The rice flail and throwing stars are well known martial art weapons and anyone found in possession will be arrested by the police. The coach must make this fact plain to all students.

Under certain circumstances, the police may decide not to prosecute a person found in possession of a weapon. This happens when the possessor is found with a martial art weapon properly secured, going directly to or from the training hall. If such a person can also produce a current Martial Arts Commission licence at the time, he may not be arrested. If, however, he is found in possession whilst having a drink in the pub next door to the training hall, or if he leaves the weapon in his car, then his defence is considerably weakened.

Conviction may also be avoided when the offending martial art 'weapon' is shown not to be a weapon. One young person made a rice flail from two bits of thin dowelling joined by lavatory chain. The police remained convinced that this was a deadly weapon. When the expert testimony tried to demonstrate how proper rice flails are used and inadvertently broke the exhibit apart, the judge accepted the distinction between a martial art weapon and a **model** of a martial art weapon. If martial art weapons are a part of your training programme, leave them in a secure place at the club. Most premises have an equipment cupboard that can be locked.

Questions

1 List as many requirements as you can for ensuring a safe training hall.
2 What precautions should you take before recommending equipment to your students?
3 Imagine that you are the chief coach of a martial art association and an accident occurs in one of your training halls. An instructor you rarely see has been negligent. Can you be taken to court?
4 How far can assistant coaches be entrusted with coaching duties?
5 What questions should an application form for membership to a club or association contain?
6 What do you do if an applicant declares a scheduled health condition that may affect her training?
7 What do you do if an applicant declares that he has previously been convicted for crimes of violence?
8 What value does a disclaimer notice have?
9 At what stage should new members apply for a Martial Arts Commission licence?
10 From what point in time does the students' M.A.C. insurance operate?
11 Why are coaches required to have a current Professional Indemnity Insurance Policy?
12 How should you match students in free- or semi-free practice?
13 Is the coach allowed to inflict unreasonable violence on a student?
14 Are two students allowed to inflict unreasonable violence upon each other if this is permitted by the rules of sparring?
15 What level of control over technique delivery is the coach supposed to show?
16 List the arrangements to be made to ensure the safety of a course or competition involving two or more clubs.
17 List two priorities to be observed when teaching martial arts to children.
18 Should you regard children as simply miniature adults?
19 What steps would you take to reduce the possibility of a child using martial art techniques in the playground?
20 Explain how a martial artist responding to an assault faces danger other than through the assault itself.
21 How can this danger be reduced?
22 Is there any circumstance in a self-defence situation where a martial artist is entitled to strike first?
23 Is the rice flail an offensive weapon?
24 How should martial art weapons be carried to and from the club?

APPENDIX 1

ORGANISATION OF
THE MARTIAL ARTS IN GREAT BRITAIN

What are the martial arts?

We all know that we practise a martial art, but what *is* a martial art?

Martial arts are quite simply systems of fighting which may additionally have sporting, self defence, or philosophical connotations.

The martial arts practised in Britain mainly come from China, Japan, Korea, Thailand and South-East Asia. Chinese martial arts are considered to be the oldest practised systems, though there is evidence that some Indian ones predate them. The Chinese arts are colloquially known as **Kung Fu**. The more correct title is **Wu Shu**.

Okinawa is one of the islands of the Ryukyu chain which effectively link Japan with the Chinese mainland. As you might expect, its martial arts are a mixture of Chinese, Japanese and indigenous practices. Karate originated in Okinawa, spreading from there to Japan.

Okinawa is known for its well developed traditional martial arts training or **Kobu-do**.

One of the earliest Japanese martial arts is **Kendo**, or 'the way of the sword'. It uses a bamboo practice sword, called a **Shinai**, and armour. The art of drawing, using and resheathing the sword is called **Iaido**.

Japanese archery or **Kyudo** is practised as a form of meditation. The nocking, drawing and loosing actions are immersed in ritual.

Traditional **Jiu Jitsu** ('the compliant way') helped the Japanese warrior to continue fighting after he lost his sword. It also equipped him to capture an enemy alive.

Aikido is 'the way of all harmony'. It is a development of jiu jitsu and, by means of joint locks and throws, it uses the opponent's strength against him.

Shorinji Kempo is a comparatively recent Japanese study of an ancient Chinese system of kung fu.

Japanese warriors studied a range of martial arts under the collective title of **Budo**.

The Korean peninsula originated three fighting systems, the first of which is named **Taekwondo** ('the way of the hand and foot'). **Tang Soo Do** is 'the way of the Chinese hand', a reference to its early origins. **Hapkido** is 'the way of all harmony'. It is quite similar to aikido and jiu jitsu.

Thai Boxing is a full contact combat sport introduced to Britain from Thailand. Full contact is the name given to a modern combat sport which uses techniques from the traditional systems.

How are the martial arts organised?

There is no law which says you must belong to a martial art organisation. Anyone can buy and wear a black belt, or have a certificate of competence printed up. This has led to problems in the past, with members of the public being deceived and perhaps injured. Martial artists realised the damage this was doing to their good name, so the more responsible groups banded together into governing bodies to set standards. Each governing body is responsible for controlling a particular martial art.

Few martial artists could tell whether those of another governing body were competent, because of the differences between the various systems. In the plethora of associations and governing bodies it became very difficult to sort the wheat from the chaff.

The logical thing to do was to form an umbrella body which which would use just one licence, one symbol and one reference point for all martial art enquiries. By banding together, the governing bodies have better representation, a buffer in the event of problems, an arbitration and a conciliation service and an insurance policy for all the licence holders. The name of the umbrella body is 'The Martial Arts Commission' and it was inaugurated in 1977.

Each governing body sends two representatives to Commission meetings and policies are decided by vote. Officers elected by governing body representatives direct the Commission's policies. Salaried staff put the agreed policies into action.

APPENDIX 2

QUALIFYING AS
A MARTIAL ARTS COMMISSION COACH

Introduction

There are basically 5 levels of classification within the Martial Arts Commission Coaching Award Scheme. The first is Assistant Coach, and the next is Coach. Everyone joining the scheme for the first time, regardless of personal grade, has to enter the scheme at either one of these two levels.

This might seem a little demeaning to start with, but just because you are personally proficient in your martial art does not automatically mean you are a good coach.

The Assistant Coach Award

Each governing body has different requirements, although the overall format is the same. Check with your governing body to see what requirements must be met. Some governing bodies require an assistant coach to be above 18 years of age and to hold at least a first degree black belt (or its equivalent). Others may require attendance at specific skill-acquisition or homologation courses as a pre-requisite of entering the award scheme. No one can enter the scheme unless they have the approval of their governing body.

All candidates must have attended a first aid course to St. John's Ordinary Standard, or to MediMAC Basic Level. Some associations arrange courses for their members; others recommend contacting the local St. John's. Check with your association secretary to see what is required in your case.

Another stringent requirement is a professional indemnity insurance policy. This is available through your association, or direct from the Martial Arts Commission's insurance brokers.

Having satisfied the governing body in these matters, the candidate coach must read this book. The information it contains provides all the resource material required to take you on to coach level.

You can also buy the National Coaching Foundation's 6 introductory study packs. See the list of useful contacts for the N.C.F.'s address, or get in touch with your association.

Next, you must enrol for a 1-day approved coaching course organised by the governing body, by the Martial Arts Commission, or by the National Coaching Foundation. Martial Arts Commission courses are attended by martial artists from various disciplines, whilst N.C.F. courses are open to the general sporting community. The information you need for the Assistant Coach Award is very general, so it really doesn't matter which course you attend. Having said that, I personally believe that governing body courses are best, because 'in-house' lecturers make more meaningful connections between coaching principles and specific practice in that particular governing body.

Contact the Martial Arts Commission or the N.C.F. for details of courses near you. Remember to take your record book, because you need the head lecturer's signature to prove you attended the right course on such and such a date. Both the Martial Arts Commission and the National Coaching Foundation can supply coaching record cards. The Commission book is particularly attractive and is obtained via your association when you first qualify under the Award Scheme. Although the actual titles of lectures may vary, the topics to be covered in a governing body or Martial Arts Commission course are:

- where the coach and club fit into the national martial art structure
- what does the coach do?
- how the coach behaves
- the coach's responsibilities
- how to screen new students
- the whys and wherefores of warm-up/cool-down
- training safety
- how to coach
- coaching and the law
- how to deal with emergencies.

Lectures covered on an N.C.F. course are:

- the coach in action
- the body in action
- safety and injury
- improving techniques
- mind over matter
- planning and practice.

Even as I write this book, Martial Arts Commission governing bodies are developing new ways to present these important topics. Coaches are practical people, and are not well suited to sitting through several hours of lectures!

The governing body may require a practical session to see whether candidates can coach effectively and safely. This is most likely to happen with newly qualified candidates assisting in their club for the first time. They may be asked to coach a small group of fellow candidates in a technique of their choosing, whilst being observed by the course examiner(s). Afterwards their performance may be discussed and helpful suggestions made on areas where improvements are necessary. No pass or fail judgement is given.

Having done all this the association will nominate its candidates to the Martial Arts Commission for certification as Assistant Coaches.

Established instructors who come late to the Award Scheme will no doubt be judged on the basis of their past performance.

When the Award Scheme is operating fully, club coaches will monitor the performance of their assistant coaches, and will put them up for qualification in exactly the same way they do for gradings.

The Coach Award

Normally, candidates to the Coach Award will be qualified assistant coaches who, following a suitable period of operation, are nominated by their club coaches to the governing body. The exception is where high grade instructors join the scheme after it has started. These may enter directly at Coach Award Level.

All candidates will already hold a current professional indemnity policy and will be of the required standard in first aid.

This time there is at least 1 full weekend course organised by the governing body or the Martial Arts Commission. This covers the following topics:

- how to get the best in terms of skill from students
- how to measure their progress
- how to improve their performance through increased fitness
- how to help students over training set-backs
- how to coach children and young people
- how to rehabilitate injured students
- how to set targets and plan training
- opening a new club (promotion and development)
- managing the club
- organising courses and events.

Your governing body may offer the alternative of attending at least four N.C.F. courses. These must cover:

- understanding and improving skill

- strength, endurance and flexibility training for the martial arts
- the prevention and rehabilitation of injury
- effective coaching.

The governing body may require attendance at additional courses, so check with it. In the interim the following general topics are on offer from the N.C.F.:

- structure of the body
- nutrition and sports performance
- developing endurance
- development of strength and speed
- developing flexibility
- an introduction to sports mechanics
- use of video in coaching
- mental preparation for performance
- the coach and athlete; working as a team
- how to plan your programme.

These lectures will be followed by a practical examination. This takes the form of a class situation in which the candidate teaches a technique to classmates whilst being observed. The coach tutor may define the techniques to be taught. Candidates' performances are itemised on an assessment sheet.
The N.C.F. is constantly reviewing its programme, so follow up your interest by contacting it via your association.
Some associations will also organise a seminar in which groups of candidate coaches are given topics to discuss and report back on.

The Senior Coach Award

Candidates for the Senior Coach Award must be long established coaches with a proven record of ability, measurable either through the technical standard of their students or through their students' consistent performances in competition. They will hold first aid qualifications and a professional indemnity policy. Selection for advancement is made by the principal/national coach of the association.
Coaching at this level is more specialised and, whilst there are N.C.F. and Martial Arts Commission courses available, the governing body is best equipped to define which areas of coaching knowledge must be investigated. One governing body may have completely different requirements from another, so it is as well to check out details.
The N.C.F. currently has the following courses on offer in selected venues throughout Britain:

- communication skills

- stress control techniques
- mechanics of sport
- how to find out more
- working with teams
- peak performance
- competitive sport and young children
- sports injury prevention and primary care.

Each course contains practical work and takes between 14 and 20 hours to complete.

The Coach Tutor Award

Coach Tutors are senior coaches nominated by their governing body. Their function is to train coaches at all levels for the association. They must be at least 30 years of age and must have practised martial art continuously over a minimum period of 10 years. As part of their governing body's structured training programme, they review in detail and expand the syllabus used for the previous 3 levels.

Once they complete these requirements satisfactorily, they will be registered with the Martial Arts Commission as coach tutors, and they will be allowed to train and qualify candidates for all levels, according to the relevant and agreed syllabus.

Principal Coach Officer

A Principal Coaching Officer is responsible for the skill training of martial artists within the association or governing body. The Principal Coaching Officer may also be referred to as the:

- National Coach
- Director of Coaching
- Chief Instructor.

The exact title is chosen by the association or governing body which confers it. In any association or governing body, the roles of Principal Coaching Officer and of Coach Tutor may be held by the same person, but this need not be the case.

APPENDIX 3

GENERAL GUIDELINES FOR COACHES TO CONSIDER WHEN ORGANISING COURSES AND EVENTS

Active coaches stage many different kinds of events for their members. The good coach knows each student involved, whether or not he is fit to take part, and if his Martial Arts Commission licence is current.

The coach operates the rules of the association and makes sure that all safety procedures are observed.

Association events are run for the entire membership, and as a coach you may be called upon to assist. All entrants will be registered with the association registrar, so verification is easy. Health monitoring cards must be checked by the organisers to ensure that no one has suffered a head injury within the past 4 weeks.

Governing body events may include entries from semi-autonomous associations. Federal governing bodies of this latter type do not deal directly with individual licence holders and participating associations are liable for ensuring the safety of their own entry.

Governing body events must use only fully qualified officials.

Open events allow participation from outside the association, so the organiser must ensure, firstly, that each person taking part is a current Martial Arts Commission licence holder and, secondly, that all are capable of working to the published rules of the event. A proper application form must be used and, because of the risk, only nationally qualified officials may be brought in.

If you teach weapons, make sure you are properly qualified by your association to do so. Only teach their usage as part of your syllabus. Limit participation to advanced students only and brief them on the dangers of carrying weapons. Do not advertise weapons' courses outside your club or association.

APPENDIX 4

A Standard Application Form

Name _____ **Date of birth** /   /

Address _____

_____

Telephone number _____

Have you ever practised a martial art?   YES/NO

If yes, please give brief details, including affiliation and grade obtained _____

_____

_____

Do you hold a current MAC licence?   YES/NO

If yes, please state by whom issued and number of licence _____

_____

Do you suffer from any of the following. Tick if yes:

Diabetes	Migraine
Epilepsy	Nervous Disorders
Haemophilia	Respiratory Problems
Heart Disorders	(eg Asthma, Hay Fever)

Have you ever been convicted of a crime of violence?   YES/NO

If yes, please give details _____

_____

_____

Do you accept that the practice of _____

involves the risk of serious injury?   **YES/NO**

Signature _____ **Date**   /   /

(Signature of parent or guardian if applicant is under 18 years)

Complete and sign this form, then send it together with 2 passport photographs and a cheque or money order for £   , payable to:

The Association reserves the right to decline your application without stating a reason.

USEFUL ADDRESSES

Martial Arts Commission 1st Floor Broadway House, 15–16 Deptford Broadway, London SE8 4PE.
Tel 01 691 3433

National Coaching Foundation 4 College Close, Beckett Park, Leeds LS6 3QH.
Tel 0532 744802

English Karate Council 1st Floor Broadway House, 15–16 Deptford Broadway, London SE8 4PE.
Tel 01 691 3433

Scottish Karate Board of Control 74 Lamington Rd, Glasgow G52 2SE.
Tel 041 883 6095

Welsh Karate Federation 'Smalldrink', Parsonage Lane, Begelly, Kilgetty.
Tel 0834 813776

Northern Ireland Karate Board 8 Four Winds Ave, Newton Park, Belfast BT8 4GF.
Tel 0232 644322

British Kung Fu Council 'Shao-lynn', 39 Tower St, King's Lynn, Norfolk.

British Taekwondo Council 9 Shrub Court, 18 Cedar Rd, Sutton, Surrey SM2 5DG.

British Jiu Jitsu Association WJJF, Barlows Lane, Fazakerley, Liverpool L9 9EH.
Tel 051 523 9611

Nippon Dai Budokai WJJF, Barlows Lane, Fazakerley, Liverpool L9 9EH.
Tel 051 523 9611

British Aikido Board 6 Halkingcroft, Langley, Slough, Berks.
Tel 075 73985

British Kendo Association Wenlock Edge, Park Hill, Pilton, Somerset BA4 4AZ.
Tel 074 989241

British Shorinji Kempo Association 32 Fairlawn Grove, Chiswick, London W4.
Tel 01 994 4324

UK Tang Soo Do Federation 44 Holden Way, Upminster, Essex RM14 1BT.
Tel 040 22 25739

UK Sulkido Federation 'National Sulkido Academy', 1st Floor, 472 Caledonian Rd, London N7 8TB.
Tel 01 627 9517

British Thai Boxing Board of Control 63 Carr Meadow, Willow Vale, Clayton Brook PR5 8HR.
Tel 0772 324935

British Students' Karatedo Federation 140 Southend Arterial Rd, Hornchurch, Essex RM2.
Tel 0708 21123

Coaching Association of Canada 333 River Rd, Ottawa, K1L BH9, Ontario, Canada.

American Coaching Effectiveness Program Box 5076, 1607 North Market, Champaign, Illinois 61820, USA.

Australian Coaching Council PO Box 176, Belconnen, ACT 2616, Australia.

Coaching Association of New Zealand PO Box 11-266, Wellington, New Zealand.

RECOMMENDED READING

I strongly recommend that all would-be coaches buy three books to cover the full spectrum of general coaching in the martial arts. This book is one of three; the others are:

Fighting Fit by David Mitchell (Unwin Paperbacks)
Health and The Martial Arts by Dr James Canney (Marshall Pickering).

In addition, there are a number of good books which will also be useful, such as the following:

Injuries in Combat Sports by G. McLatchie (Offox)
Sports Fitness and Sports Injuries edited by Thomas Reilly (Faber)
Competition Karate by Hamish Adam and Greg McLatchie (A & C Black).

INDEX